Your Boots
Our Books

Boots
for Books

ACADEMIC
PATRIOTISM

Carl R. Boyd

AMERICAN STUDENTS STRIVING FOR EXCELLENCE IN HONOR OF OUR
UNITED STATES ARMED FORCES

Published by Purpose Publishing
1503 Main Street #168 ❧ Grandview, Missouri
www.purposepublishing.com

ISBN: 978-0-6922900-2-6

Cover design by: Thaddeus Jordan
Editing by: Frank Kresen
Interior Design: LaToya Humes

Printed in the United States of America

TABLE OF CONTENTS

The End

Every American student *must* strive for excellence, in school, out of respect for every American serviceman and woman who gets hurt, hospitalized or killed to defend the rights, and opportunities, for every American student to attend school.

And, every American school – that is, *every* American school: public, private, parochial, charter, independent, alternative, home, combinations thereof, and other; *every* American school – *must* be excellent for the very same reason.

Praise for *Academic Patriotism*

"You should read this book. Mr. Boyd has done a fantastic job. I don't know where he got all these great ideas."

> Gerald Caldwell
> Commander
> VFW Post 8100 Grandview, Missouri

"Reading Carl Boyd's book is like listening to him talk, directly, to you. Academic Patriotism is a wonderful conversation."

> Barb Friedmann, Founder
> Coalition for Community
> Collaboration/ Community Together

"I am not on the show (Boyd's Academic Patriotism radio talk show) to promote the book. I'm just proud to be associated with Carl Boyd and the work he's doing. But, it is an excellent book."

> Ron Miller
> Decorated Vietnam Veteran

"The program can have a tremendous impact in bridging the gap of youth and community. It is an enhancement to any school curriculum..."

> from Foreword by
> Carl N. Tate, Sr. Command Sergeant
> Major U.S. Army - Retired

"Uncle Carl's book is a blessing to our family, including my son and daughter-in-law, Edmon and India Daniels who are currently stationed at Beale Air Force Base in Marysville, California. When he dropped off my personal copy of the book at work, there were co-workers who insisted that he return, the same day, with copies for them. This is a true story."

Foreword

The Stoots for Boots Campaign in my opinion is one of the best programs to come along to inspire young people to be all they can be. The program helps them to understand the sacrifices veterans have made for our country, and how sacrificing for others can give one great personal satisfaction and pride.

When Stoots for Boots Campaign was implemented at Ruskin High School in the Hickman Mills School District in Kansas City Missouri, veterans were asked to interact with the Junior ROTC Cadets. As veterans we considered it an honor and privilege to share with this amazing group of young people who show great potential for leadership. Veterans shared experiences of courage, discipline, and commitment to a cause much greater than themselves.

This program can have a tremendous impact in bridging the gap of youth and community. It is an enhancement to any school curriculum to encourage students to strive for excellence in any endeavor of their choosing.

Carl N. Tate Sr.
Command Sergeant Major
U.S. Army- Retired

For TEACHERS -
A Curriculum Guide
For STUDENTS -
A Study Guide
For PARENTS -
An InvolvementGuide

For Troops -
A Mentoring Guide
For America -
A Must!

Acknowledgements

"Wonderful Wanda" Boyd, my adorable wife, endured my absence (in the room where I write at home) for hours at a time as I worked on this book; and, much of the time we shared in conversation has been about the "STOOTS for Boots" Campaign. This is not the first time she has been so gracious, and I love her for this and much more.

"The First 28"

The following list contains the names of students who deserve both a "Thank you" and "Congratulations!" These are the Ruskin Senior High School students who made a statement of commitment to veterans who came to their school Thursday May 15, 2014 for the press conference that was called, specifically, for this reason. The "Thank you" is for stepping up and making this pledge directly to American veterans whose hands they shook, as they said: "Because of your sacrifice to defend our nation, I am serious about my education." They are to be congratulated for being the first 28 American students for making the commitment in this formal and public way. They are:

Jerome Asbury

Precious Awopetu

Mariah Barnes

Ryan Beaver

Sinia Caceres

Katrina Carter

Patricia Charles

Sunny Cisneros

Antonio Collier

Derric Durham

Decorey Forshee-Harris

Markesia Gates

Ciara Griffin

Naomi Hill

Tyteona Jenkins

Alexis Johnson

Jiamyiah Jordan

Lanesha Kimbrel

Jackie Lowery

Corinn Mason

Byron Miller

Jerica Palmer

Janine Pedrosa

Breanna Stevenson

Lazapay Wandick

Kristal Whitaker

Bre'A Williams

Shardae Williams

A resounding "Thank you" to those on the receiving end of the students' statements: to all Americans who wear, and all who have worn, a uniform in a branch of service in our United States Armed Forces!

Direct Involvement

I was blessed to have outstanding associates directly involved in the finishing of this book and the launching of the "STOOTS for Boots" Campaign. A big thank you to Michelle Gines and Purpose Publishing for taking a chance on my writing and for believing in the concept. Thanks to Frank W. Kresen for painstakingly editing the very challenging offering that includes my peculiar writing style. For the "STOOTS for Boots" logo that appears on the cover page, much appreciation goes to Cristina Shell for her artistry and her patience. Chris Evans of T-Shirt King in Kansas City placed Cristina's logo on the T-Shirts handed out by veterans to Ruskin Senior High School students on September 11, 2014. Mr. Evans will continue to provide "STOOTS" attire. Carrie Stapleton is president of Phillips-West Public Relations and Celeste Reed is Ms. Stapleton's partner. Phillips-West Public Relations coordinated the press conference that was held to "kick off" the campaign. The event was held on May 15, 2014 at Ruskin Senior High School. The school and the Hickman Mills School District expressed appreciation for the firm's involvement. We are indebted to them for their expertise and commitment. Thanks to the Hickman Mills School District superintendent, Dr. Dennis Carpenter and Ruskin Senior High principal, Jesse Rivers. Kudos to Colonel Ivan Glasco (USMC Retired), JROTC Drill Instructor at Ruskin, for constructing and conducting, the program at the press conference. To decorated Vietnam veteran, Ron Miller, thank you for organizing the military guests who received the students' statements of commitment on that day. To Carl Tate (Sgt. Major Retired), 5th District Commander, VFW, I express my gratitude for support and service. To my daughter, Dr. Alisha Malloy, who graduated from Annapolis with honors and served six years in the Navy, I cannot say enough about your patience with me, your guidance and your continued commitment to this concept but, more so, to our country. As always (you can check every book I've written) thank you to my Vice President (the "Chief"), Ruth Jones who has been with me from "Day 1" of my stepping out on Faith to work with schools in 1986. Much appreciation for the Spiritual and technical involvement in this project goes to my niece, La

Faye ("La Family") Daniels and to my nephews, Eric, Erun and Edmon. Cheryl Brown Henderson, an historic icon (Brown v. Topeka), has shown support and provided sage advice towards the completion of the book. A debt of gratitude remains, always, towards Dr. Karen Young for clearing the way for the use of the Educator's Edge series, Challenges And Champions, and to Dr. Jerry George for the development of the series in 1998. To business manager, Pat Lantz and the Student Press@ DeLaSalle, in Kansas City, Missouri for print designs for correspondence from the campaign. Ms. Marquita Miller helps with ideas for financing and with ongoing support. Thank you, so much, Ms. Miller. For all videos, thank you Kerwyn Looney. For all music, thank you Luther Wilson. Thanks to Donna O. Johnson and Y.C. Chen for providing their Guaranteed A+ Plus model of study which proves that serious students can decide to excel and do so.

Significant Support

The oft-quoted statement, "I'm afraid that, if I start naming those who have helped me, I am bound to leave out someone", is one clearly understood by this author. Whenever, and however, I can make up for omissions I'll certainly do all I can. Listed below, alphabetically, are supporters who, literally, made it possible for "Wonderful Wanda" and me to keep going during the writing of this work:

Elbert Anderson	Ken "Chief" Hill
David Blaise	Rev. Robert Hill
Valencia Broadus	Ollie Hubbard
Alvin Brooks	Karla Jackson
Doris E. Bantom-Brown	Marvetta Johns
Thomas J. Brown	Calvin Jones
Annette Bush	Floyd Jones
Charles Bush	John Martin Jones
Jannette Bush	Nicki Jones

Misha Bush

Kerry & Tynette Butler

A.J. Byrd

Drs. James & Angel Byrd

Chuck Byrd

Dr. & Mrs. Artis & Gail Clark

Lee & Rosie Lee Clark

Lovette Clark

Wade & Carmelita Clark

("Big John") & Dr. Edith Coleman

Melba Curls

Dyan Devereaux

Leon Dixon

Erika Dodson

Naeema A. El-Scari

Natasha Ria El-Scari

Carl Evans

Kenneth & Peggy Ford

Marlowe Garlington

Teresa Habernal

Carolyn Hall

Rev. Glenn & Emma J. Hancock

Mike & Mae Hancock

Musudeen Harrell

Danise Hartsfield

Rev. Wallace S. Hartsfield

Alisa Henley

Rev. Antoine Lee

Debra J. Lee

John Little

Gary & Willetta McGhee

Calvin Neal

Carlos Nelson

Jerry Nelson

James Nunnelly

Dewanna Oguinn

Josie Padilla

Gregory Patton II

Clyde & Claudette Rogers

Curtis Rogers

Samuel & Gloria Shareef

John Shields

Dawna Shumate

Rodney & Stephenie Smith

Joseph & Rhetta Taylor

James & Emma Venn

Pastors Calvin & Cassandra Wainright

Reginald Wallace

Karen Williams

Luvenia Williams

DeQuai Wilson

Dr. Susan Wilson

Prologue
The Campaign

The **STOOTS For Boots Campaign** is a simple effort to get American students, "from sea to shining sea", to dedicate their effort in class to the men and women of America's Armed Forces, veteran, reserve and active duty. The acronym, **STOOTS,** stands for **S**tudents' **T**heater **O**f **O**perations, **T**he **S**chool. The connotation, here, is to introduce this campaign's call for "patriotic parallelism." As military personnel confront theaters of war with serious purpose, so should students, in a parallel way, confront classrooms and laboratories with the same sense of serious purpose.

Merriam-Webster sites the following definitions for the terms, Theater Of War and Theater Of Operations:

Theater Of War – the entire land, sea, and air area that is or may become involved directly in war operations.

Theater Of Operations – the part of a theater of war in which active combat operations are conducted.

A school district may be considered akin to a "theater of war" – perhaps, a theater of education. The district determines the subject matter that is appropriate for instruction, based upon the philosophy of education agreed upon among district administrators directed by the community the district serves. The philosophy and subject matter of American school districts are consistent with the educational goals of our nation. A school may, then, be considered the part of the district where "active operations (teaching and learning) are conducted." We see them as analogous to war theaters of operation because the same enemies we confront in warfare are teaching their children to outperform us academically. And, where schools are concerned, we have many more foreign competitors, even among "friends", than those we find on battlefields.

If we are successful at convincing young Americans to take school as seriously as their military counterparts take defending our nation, we should be able, also, to help them see that their responsibility towards preserving our nation's future in the classroom is a lot easier than preserving our nation's freedoms on the battlefield. This being the case, students have no excuse for failing to uphold their end of the patriotic equation by, at least, attending school regularly, and making every attempt to excel. They should do this (STOOTS says, "they *must*" do this) in honor of those who have the far more difficult task of facing "dangers, toils and snares" in foreign lands, against well-armed enemies, whose aim is to destroy what these true American heroes are dying to preserve.

During this year, 2014, there appears to be a greater degree of respect for America's military than the nation has seen in many decades. Human interest stories about families' surprise reunions with service personnel returning home from distant lands fill network and local news time slots. There are numerous campaigns, funds and activities pledging support for all who have worn, and who presently wear, the uniforms that represent our nation's defense. In some cases the efforts are ceremonial; in some cases, temporary. In some cases where the efforts are permanent, there are continuous calls for members, volunteers and support, as it is difficult to ever get quite enough. There are many – indeed, millions of – American citizens looking for ways to express their support for our military. This book shows how year-round involvement with schools supports our military heroes.

Book 1:

The Pride

We are proud
American PATS

Parents **A**dministrators **T**eachers **S**tudents
An Inseparable Alliance

Parents Administrators Teachers Students
An Inseparable Alliance

Parents, Administrators, Teachers and Students are natural allies. While some see the acronym, "PATS", as an abbreviation for "patriots" – which is also true of this "natural alliance" who form the American school community – this reference congratulates the millions of Parents, Administrators, Teachers and Students who work together everyday to make American academic patriotism a reality in honor of American troops

Because this truth does not seem to command the large audiences that competitive media desire, positive stories about the strength of school teams are often neglected. Historically, Parents have depended upon school Administrators and staff to serve as surrogate parents. Teachers know that their success depends upon Students' success, and the possibilities for students to succeed are enhanced where there is a good home-school partnership. Students fare well when they realize that their parents/guardians and school personnel are in agreement; not only sharing a common belief system but also carrying out a cooperative action plan to achieve academic excellence and social harmony. Perhaps because this unity of function occurs so regularly across America, it is not seen as particularly newsworthy. Perhaps the academic patriotism context will help.

Our Armed Forces would be proud to see the ways schools emulate the comradeship that is the rule for military units whose very lives depend upon cooperation and high expectations. "Would be" proud does not suggest that this unity does not already exist among parents, administrators, teachers and students in many schools throughout the United States. It means that we have not shared, with our valiant warriors, how much they inspire schools to function as a team. We have not publicized the degree to which military analogies have marked our approach to helping school teams understand the level of efficiency we desire to reach. The pride of warriors cannot hide when the uniform enters an arena. It is time that our PATS pride is never missed when anyone enters an American school. American military uniforms command respect with the wearing. American schools should command respect with the entering.

To declare that parents, administrators, teachers and students are an inseparable alliance is to state a simple matter of fact. To suggest that the inseparable nature of this alliance is always positive is to be unreasonably optimistic. While bound by singularity of purpose and coincidence of geography, we cannot make the assumption that all involved with our schools will be cooperative. Natural allies, yes. Automatic companions, not necessarily. Those who readily identify with the title of this first chapter, **We Are Proud American PATS, An Inseparable Alliance,** are those whose understanding and demonstration of American academic patriotism must be presented to the entire nation as the norm we seek in all of our schools. We are not all "there" yet, but we are asking all American parents, administrators, teachers and students to form the positive, cooperative, alliances in your communities that will make your country proud. Let our pride be the, genuine, humble, acceptance of our singular and collective responsibilities to help schools preserve our future. As an inseparable alliance, all **PATS** have roles.

Chapter 1
P: **Parents** As Patriotic Allies

Allow me a few chapter titles from a book I use for a school-parenting Sunday school class, *Bible-Based Family Schooling*[1]. There are three titles, of 49, that will help to explain my view of parents' roles based upon their relationships with other members of the school team/alliance.

First, let us consider, *Where Adults Believe, Children Achieve.* My belief in belief, as the starting point in developing effective schools, is as important for the home as for the school. In addressing the preparation for a successful school experience for students, I have discussed, in Book 2, **Excellence Is a Choice**, the importance of school leaders getting staff "on board" so that they can greet parents as a united front. Parents need to know what a school stands for to help their children succeed within the context of the school's mission, long range goals, rules of conduct and outline of cooperative interaction among all in that school family. But, the belief system of a school (a district, a state) is hard-pressed to overcome a lack of belief in the home. In effective schools we generally find serious parents passionately asserting that their children must go to an effective (excellent) school because "My child is excellent." Parents are welcome allies to administrators and staff when they, too, are believers.

Next, there is this: *Adults Set Trends For Children And Friends.* We hear about peer pressure among adolescents and teens, and most often the reference is negative. Today's world of technology causes us to be concerned about our children "getting farther away from us," as they separate themselves from parents and from "normal", human, modes of communication. And, again, media seem to emphasize our being disconnected from youth more than our being tied to them. Parents' rhetoric includes such phrases as: "I don't know where this music comes from." "They need a curfew. There's no need for teens to be out of the house after 10:00 p.m. during the week, or, certainly, midnight on weekends." "I can't understand a word they're saying when they call themselves talking to each other." Oops! That was in the 60's. "My bad."

The fact is that now, as was true in "our day" – name any era – young people want, and need, adult guidance. They want, and seek, adult approval. And, contrary to what some reality TV presentations would have us believe young people are more concerned about being accepted in their homes than elsewhere. When teens are guided to complain about having "nothing to do" they are implying that the adults upon whom they depend are not providing anything for them. Of course, the statements are made after they come from school, band, football practice, soccer tryouts, a student council pizza party, a local talent search "open mike", a trip to the museum, the zoo or the Lego competition championships, night hoops basketball, a college tour, roller skating or some other activity sponsored, prepared and conducted by adults.

Please know that children "are supposed to" complain about adults. Didn't we? A difference in the trend, however, seems to be that adults are yielding to teen pressure more than teens are yielding to peer pressure. As true trendsetters, adults can join our military in setting standards of excellence, and accepting nothing less. *And, accepting nothing less!* What happened to the dropout whose trousers sagged and whose self esteemed sagged even more? The language he used when addressing school staff was not appropriate, and his parents were in a quandary as to how to make him behave. What happened to this "problem child"? You cannot tell me that was him I saw visiting the principal, this morning, standing tall, using standard English, saying, "Yes ma'am" and "Yes sir", wearing his trousers properly creased as part of the military uniform that lets us know, just by looking at this new young adult, that someone would accept nothing less. Military recruits do not set trends for their branches of service. They are led. They follow. Children must not set trends for adults. They must be led. They must follow.   Children crave adult guidance. They will follow.

Finally, *The Children's Education Is the Parents' Vocation.* Where children are in attendance, the entire family is enrolled. Children must not be allowed to attend school alone; first, because they need help, but, most importantly, because it is a family's responsibility to be a part of the experience.

Students who make a habit of discussing, with their parents, what happened in school, everyday, tend to try to make something happen in school, everyday. This is especially true when the children know that a parent who is not satisfied with the report will contact the school to find out why nothing is happening. We often hear educators express a desire for parents (for guardians) to get "more involved" in school. We understand what they mean. Actually, parents and guardians are always "involved." The issue is whether they are involved in children's success or in their failure. For instance, parents who express no concern about "what happened in school, today" are parents who are very involved in creating a child who is disengaged from school.

Some parents may *work* two, perhaps, three jobs to make household ends meet. All parents *have* one job to make children's ends "neat." Single adults with no children will make sure to provide food, shelter, clothing, transportation and modes of communication for themselves. Whatever else goes on in their lives, they attend to some basics that are imperative to address. Sometimes, "things get slow", and work is hard to come by. However they manage it, they will find ways to survive physically, and, therefore also psycho-emotionally, by whatever means necessary. This sometimes, means having more than one job. When marriage and children are added to the equation, the same imperative is present; but, even more so with the responsibility for someone else.

I know that there are legitimate exceptions. Sometimes circumstances prevent a person – even a family – from enjoying a healthy, wholesome lifestyle. One of the real reasons for studying hard in school is to research how to end poverty. Our attitudes concerning well being for ourselves, and for our children, must include the need to make a way for those who follow us to enjoy better lives than we. We must also understand our responsibility to our society for helping to create a social climate that is conducive to safety and productivity. We want this for our families, for our communities, for our country. Our heroes fight for it. Our children must study to preserve it. We must be integral parts of their study, as examples of concerned guardians who express a desire for children to be successful in school, and as participatory parents of our nation's future, as allies with educators, for as long as we have children in school. A title I did not use, above, from my family schooling book; is one that is self -explanatory. The title: *When Parents Cooperate, Schools Can Operate.* Thanks to all cooperating parents.

Chapter 2
A: Administrators As Patriotic Allies

As I continue to contemplate the "ally analogy", using our Armed Forces for inspiration and as living examples of allies in action, it occurs to me that military personnel negotiating our relationships with allies around the world, have to be able to take for granted that they certainly have allies, at home, working diligently in our schools. They have to know, by our actions, that we are studying their exemplary leadership and developing ways to make them more comfortable upon their return from duty than they were before they left. That's one of the things that allies do. Those in our schools who understand this better than most are school administrators.

Stephen R. Covey wrote *The 7 Habits of Highly Effective People.* Shamelessly borrowing from his title, I have titled a presentation I've been allowed to make to school administrators throughout America, *Seven Principals With Highly Effective Habits.* I did not, at the time, use the ally factor as a foundation for citing their habits, but upon revisiting my notes containing their attributes, I can point out why the "good ally" analogy fits them quite well. Their attitudes, aptitude and conduct (habits) do not only make them good allies to **P**arents, **T**eachers and **S**tudents, but through their leadership they help those around them become better allies to one another.

I selected these seven principals for three reasons. My first reason for including these particular principals was because of their competence. Reason two is based upon being able to identify seven distinct qualities I wanted to discuss even as interaction with each of them taught me that many of their attributes overlapped or could be interchangeable. Reason number three is based upon the fact that I did, in fact, have opportunities to interact with each of them. Alphabetically, they are:

1. Principal: Robert D. Brazil

Habit: Supporting His Staff

My interaction with Dr. Robert D. Brazil occurred at Parkside Elementary School on the south side of Chicago. He was principal when I was the 7th and 8th-grade science teacher. While I was an experienced teacher – having taught for seven years before going over to Parkside – I was observed by the principal when I began at Parkside in the same manner as would be required of any new teacher coming into the profession. In his counseling session with me, after his observation of my teaching (my classroom decorum, my lesson introduction, lesson development, interaction with students, classroom management, use of materials and – "back in the day" before Smart Boards – use of the chalkboard, my care, confidence and consistency, etc.) he said something that was very inspiring. Dr. Brazil said to me, "If you have a creative idea, I'll find the budget for its implementation."

Upon hearing those words, my ego told me that I must have made some kind of impression on my new principal. Further interaction with that principal and the staff revealed to me that I was not the only teacher at Parkside who heard those words.

Some might think that having such a "blank check" might cause a staff member to come up with something frivolous just to use whatever funds were made available. Actually, the opposite is true. With that kind of confidence in, and support for, a staff member from the school's leader, one then takes the utmost care in presenting sound ideas so as to show that confidence was well placed. Another way to express this, in our current context, is to say that it creates in staff members a desire to become good, strong, allies.

2. Principal: Reggie Brown

Habit: Leading "Instructionally"

Any study of effective schools, by whatever contemporary nomenclature, includes the essentiality of having an instructional leader. Reggie Brown was principal at one of Chicago's largest schools, Chicago Vocational School (CVS). At the time, in the mid-1970s – CVS enrolled 4800 daytime students and an additional 800 evening attendees. When Brown arrived he was greeted with students shooting dice on the front steps in front of marijuana smoking onlookers. Staff morale was low, and students' in-class conduct was in need of an adjustment.

When Reggie Brown invited – yes, invited – his staff to meet with him at 6:30 a.m., at least a half-hour before students arrived, their attendance was close to 100%. One of the main reasons for their cooperation was due to his promise of teaching teachers how to teach, and how to manage their classrooms. He was a leader in instruction, by instruction, and by example. He did not invite staff into a session with guest speakers. He did not set up a climate designed to embarrass ineffective teachers. He rolled up his sleeves, went to the chalkboard, demonstrated techniques and

31

visited classrooms when asked (or, when he saw the need) to demonstrate the tenets of what the school was (under his leadership) about.

As the first Director of Chicago's PUSH For Excellence Program, sponsored by Operation PUSH[2], in 1976, Reggie Brown taught staff and students what the program stood for and its chief tenets. One afternoon between classes, he asked me to point out a student. I asked, "Any student?" He said, "Any student." Remember, CVS had 4800 daytime students. There were hundreds in the hall. I pointed out a young man standing at his locker. Dr. Brown said, "Phillip." I'm thinking how fortuitous that I happened to point in the direction of a student whose name was known to the principal. Phillip said, "Yessir." Reggie Brown said, "Tell Mr. Boyd what PUSH for Excellence is about." Phillip responded, "We must attend school every day, arriving on time and participating in class. We must study two hours a night. We must sign a contract that says we will do these things, stay out of gangs and have no children before graduating from high school. Our parents must exchange phone numbers with our teachers, promise to be involved with our education and sign a contract that says they understand, and will abide by, these tenets."

Brown took a gold CVS lapel pin from his pocket and pinned the student while saying, "Good job." (He told me to point at "a student" out of hundreds). There have been many sessions on how to define Instructional Leadership. This kind of instructional leadership makes students ("Phillip, an' 'em"), staff (volunteering to come to school at 6:30 a.m.) and parents (exchanging phone numbers with teachers) the strongest of allies.

3. Principal: Anita Dortch

Habit: Providing for Professional Development

In the same spirit as Dr. Robert D. Brazil finding a budget for a good idea, Dr. Anita Dortch found ways to expose her staff, at Lakeside Middle School in Fort Wayne, Indiana, to consistent professional development exposure. In the same spirit as Dr. Reggie Brown had me to "Point out a student", Dr. Dortch had students line up and greet me, as their guest, with quotes from materials and concepts passed on to the staff by session leaders from outside of Lakeside. The evidence of how strong an alliance parents, administrators, teachers and students shared was manifest in the openness with which all involved received, and implemented, fresh ideas.

A testimony to their trust in each other was their receptiveness to "outsiders" with no cynicism, no suspicion or resistance in front of their peers. Dr. Dortch had a staff comprised of administrators and teachers who, apparently, knew what strategies fit their campus and how to pass on to the students the elements that were compatible with their belief system(s) and school culture. If we can believe that you can gain insight into a school's leadership based upon the collective personalities of the students, I'd have to say that Lakeside gets very high marks. The friendliness of the students, as they shared their remarks and their confidence, spoke to the team concept that exists at the school. Schools open to continuous professional development, always seeking to improve, are schools where staff and students function as allies within the schools, and where they make allies of those invited to assist with their professional growth.

4. Principal: Neely Dunn

Habit: Welcoming Parents

The parents who volunteered at McNair Middle School in Cocoa, Florida looked as though they were members of the staff. This was not only because of their appearance and professional conduct, but also because of the way McNair's staff received them. All seemed comfortable treating each other with the utmost respect. Their interaction appeared to be naturally congenial with no extra effort required to see each other as equals. Neely Dunn after reading this paragraph might say, "And?"

The suggestion of someone conducting in-service sessions on parental involvement at McNair Middle School would probably be similar to someone suggesting that we give lessons on flying to eagles. Parents seemed to be as much a part of the school as were all of the other "allies." With the professionalism of the staff, a visitor would not be surprised at the attitudes and aptitudes of students. But, the presence of parents who regularly shared an equal partnership among all who played roles in the school's success could have nothing less than a positive impact on the school climate.

Parents new to the school who met Neely Dunn for the first time must have known, immediately, that they and their children had an ally. This was, and is, altogether appropriate. All functioning for the advance of "their" (the entire team's) children, both academically and socially, made parents, administrators and teachers natural allies. The strength of the alliance depends upon the mutuality of respect and willingness to work together among team members. Seeing the example of adult cooperation and congeniality, students had, both, a model to emulate and an incentive to follow suit as they, too, felt like, and were treated as, allies.

The purpose of this writing is to encourage American educators and American students to be "warriors for learning" in a vein similar to the way our military heroes are warriors for liberty. The appeal is not to, just, follow their examples to achieve excellence; but to pursue excellence *because of* their examples. Military recruits with no initial familial or, even, geographic ties to one another become fast allies through basic training. It must be basic to children's training that their parents become fast allies of their teachers. This can happen, effectively, when the school administration welcomes all – the students, their parents, and school staff – as natural, and equal allies.

5. Principal: Curtis Rogers

Habit: Engaging Community Resources

"A new TV?" "A new ten-speed bicycle?!?" "A trip to the Grand Canyon!" "Groceries for a family of eight!!" "A new wardrobe for the children?"

These gifts and raffle awards came after the announcements of scholarships and advanced learning tools. This was just another graduation at Fairview Alternative School in Kansas City, Missouri, where Curtis Rogers was principal.

Teachers at many schools did not want "these problem kids" on their campuses. For many of the students, Fairview was their last (academic) chance. Major, international, conferences (e.g., The Annual "Challenging Learners With Untapped Potential – *Students At-Risk'"* – Conference in Phoenix, Arizona) are held to address how schools should confront students who fit Fairview's profile. Rogers was in attendance at such conferences. He should have been the convener. Not only could he have demonstrated his no-nonsense approach towards helping difficult students reform, but, he could have shown schools and school districts how to tap into myriad community resources that are very often overlooked.

Visitors who attended graduation ceremonies and/or awards programs at Fairview Alternative School probably thought that the articles presented to students and family members were special acquisitions for singular moments. Perhaps, as gifts and prizes, the major items were saved for only certain occasions. The important consideration is that the grantors of the magnificent bounty did not "show up" the evening before the occasion. Relationships were being cultivated, year-'round, by a school principal who helped all stakeholders to understand that the term means "we all have a stake" in what happens with our youth. As important as the items were to the recipients and those who, observing the activities, would work towards earning same next year; the importance of the items did not compare to the importance of the allies.

Effective alternative school educators all share a common plight. Students sent to you to "straighten up" so they could return, reformed, to the sending school, do not want to leave the alternative. There are many reasons for this, not the least of which are things such as safety and order, rigor and relevance, a caring staff, challenges to students to find their "better selves", high expectations, and among other things, effective leadership. In all categories, I could use Curtis Rogers as the example. Here, I am discussing cultivating allies. Please know that the reactions to receiving great gifts and awards by students and their parents are, at least, matched by the feelings in the hearts of those who present them. They are convinced, as school allies led by a wise leader, that their presence – more than their presents – is crucial to helping students discover that they'd rather be recognized for their positive accomplishments than feared because of their negative reputations.

Please know that there are human resources near you who are more than willing to join your team. Sometimes it means just being asked. Sometimes it means keeping eyes and hearts open for overtures you might, otherwise, miss. Oftentimes it means publicizing existing relationships in ways that cause others to desire similar relationships.

I don't know which came first, "the chicken or the 'beg'", but the treat offered and, then, accepted, or the treat requested and, then, provided have the same result during, and before, graduation. All in attendance know that you have an alliance that enhances all aspects of student matriculation. Curtis Rogers. Community Resources. Capital Results.

6. Principal: Marcia Spiller

Habit: Being a Family Member

At the time – in the late 1990s – The Children's School in Atlanta, Georgia had 523 elementary students. I guess that explains it. It was not a huge campus so it's no wonder that Dr. Spiller knew all the children's names, birthdays and family situations. When she asked one student, "How did your grandmother's operation go?" and said to another student, "Happy Birthday", it should have been no surprise. Principals of smaller schools do that. Donna Burch, in Kansas City, wished her students, "Happy Birthday".

Actually, I was fortunate to have met some excellent administrators. Reggie Brown at CVS in Chicago said, "Point out a student." He knew the name of my random selection. Donna Burch knew students' birthdays. Marcia Spiller was aware of students' family situations. What made these leaders special was not their fantastic memories but their genuine engagement.

As I was allowed to tour the grounds of The Children's School campus, I was impressed with what I saw; and, it was not just structures and equipment. Some of us recall the days of, "Oh-oh, here comes the principal." Something significant – usually, negative – must have been going on to get the principal out of the office. This rare "sighting" struck fear in the hearts and minds of even innocent children hoping that they were not in trouble. Children at what was, truly, "the children's school", were not only comfortable in Marcia Spiller's presence; but, seemed genuinely happy to see her. She took time to listen to their informal exchanges and if she inquired, "How is your dad?", they knew that she really wanted to know.

To be an ally of your school community residents goes further than wanting "your school" to do well in science and technology fairs and athletic events. Principals who want "their children" to do well are concerned about the whole child and the whole of the child's family. This concern manifests at a personal level when the principal is a part of the family. The only way for the other school allies – again, the parents, teachers and students – to feel the authenticity of this relationship is for the school leader to be an exemplar of its reality.

I write about principals with highly effective habits. These administrators have been effective because their attributes were, and are, habits. I chose to mention Marcia Spiller's habit of being family among her students and their parents. I could certainly write about her knowledge, her professionalism, her resume, her management skills; or, any number of additional competencies. Here, I am addressing a particular characteristic in each of seven outstanding principals. Many of their gifts are interchangeable. But, in my effort to illustrate the different ways administrators can assume their roles in the Parents, Administrators, Teachers and Students alliance, I called upon my recollection of distinct skill sets for illustration. There are many other principals I can cite for their excellence, but these seven habits are analogous to principals' military-style efficiency exhibited in America's Armed Forces; not necessarily as an intentional design; but certainly in the excellence of outcome. But, as it relates to projecting academic patriotism, this call goes beyond needing American schools to be excellent. We need leaders who form alliances with, and within, their units. Leaders such as:

7. Principal: Karen Williams

Habit: Consistent Feedback

In every classroom, everyday, every teacher was observed in class by principal, Dr. Karen Williams. It was inevitable that Dr. Williams would become district superintendent, but as principal of Cordova Middle School in the Alhambra District, Phoenix, Arizona, she left no teacher – and, by extension, no student or parent/guardian – in the dark as to how they were progressing in their roles. Dr. Williams did not have an assigned time to visit each teacher, day-to-day. But, all teachers and students knew that before the day was over, they would see their principal, and their principal would see them.

As important as the visit was, the consistency of the behavior was, at least, equally important. Military personnel do not function in the dark as it pertains to chain of command. There is no greater illustration of discipline and order, in the entire world, than that found in the United States Armed Forces. Conducting the business of education with similar efficiency results in high academic achievement, exemplary codes of conduct and the establishment of traditions that cause parents to look forward to having all of their children attend "that" school.

Who are we, American schools? There should be one, consistent, response to that question. We are the best in the world. We understand the importance of exemplifying the consistent manifestation and preservation of "life, liberty and the pursuit of happiness" through continually improving the academic levels of succeeding generations who use what they are taught to lead the world to righteousness. Administrators in American schools must accept nothing less. And, as lifelong learners, themselves, they must surround themselves with likeminded allies. Their passion for cooperative competence, requiring that all in the school family see themselves as natural allies in the pursuit of excellence should be infectious throughout the school community. It has certainly been the case for these seven – and the 70s of sevens who are too seldom supported to the degree that they deserve. Let us all become cooperative allies to them, as they are allies to our children and our troops.

Chapter 3
T: Teachers As Patriotic Allies

Teaching is the profession that launches all others. However lucrative the career, however high the office, however influential the position, however enjoyable the work, those who sit in lofty seats stand on the shoulders of teachers.

The everyday, hands-on, motivation, instruction, evaluation, and feedback responsibilities for keeping the PATS alliance together falls squarely on the shoulders of America's teachers.

There are times when some **parents** are negligent. This is, of course, unfair to, both, teachers and (most of all) to the children of those very parents. But, while there are true cases of parental neglect, dedicated teachers throughout America must, still, assume responsibility, everyday, for student instruction.

Some **administrators** may exhibit none of the "seven effective habits" cited above, or any other characteristic of professional leadership. But, while school communities and local boards of education are taking measures to transition out ineffective leaders, dedicated teachers must appear before their students every morning with the attitude that all is as it should be for the students to thrive.

All American **students** are not "All-American" students. Some students take more time than others to "come around" when it comes to understanding their importance in the PATS alliance, and acquitting themselves accordingly. But, while some students are slow to show what they know, dedicated teachers must continue to treat them with high expectations for the achievement levels that will emerge "when the light comes on."

Wherever else lines are "blurry" (e.g., negligent parents, ineffective administrators, difficult students), teachers must clear up all things that tend to interfere with students' understanding of subject matter and practice of proper learning conduct, consistent with academic patriotism. The central focal point of academic patriotism is the student. The primary facilitator of academic patriotism is the classroom teacher. School structures vary and change. There are "normal" public schools. There are alternative schools. There are charter schools, parochial schools, private schools, magnet schools, home schools and others. Whatever the structure, nomenclature or system, the one constant that defines a place called "school" is students and teachers. Students may have the "luxury" of sometimes being mediocre. Teachers must always be exemplary.

The greatness of American schools depends upon the efficiency with which the alliance performs. An understanding by all other alliance members of the imperative of efficiency, coupled with their performance complementing that understanding, gives teachers the support they need to get the job done in the classroom. Whatever else occurs, even if team members "feel good" about their unity, when American students are not achieving at high academic levels, the "feel good" experience is meaningless.

There was a time, "back in the day", when teachers were perceived as surrogate parents and were, consequently, given "free rein" to discipline children almost as they saw fit. Parents granted them the moral authority to help raise their children. The introduction of a more enlightened era has seen the reduction of teachers' near absolute authority. Teachers were admonished to abandon corporal punishment in favor of more interactive strategies between parents, students and staff. They were, and are, cautioned to avoid (even the appearance of) abuse of the authority – physical and psychological – that they still have, today. Now, there are those who think that we pushed the discipline pendulum too far in the tolerant direction and determined that we must enact conduct codes of "zero tolerance." Therefore, on one hand, teachers are directed to tolerate no suggestion of an offense. On the other hand, American teachers are subject to lawsuits and "viral video" should a reprimand give any hint of being too harsh.

It is well that the "free rein" era ended. It existed at a time when close-knit communities demanded that all adults – not just parents and teachers, but all adults– exercise authority over the neighborhood children. Neighborhoods functioned in that manner in "that day". We do realize that we live in "a new day." But, whatever time it is, we must allow teachers to be teachers. They do not need to be police officers, school psychologists (though to a limited degree, it is part of their profession), armed protectors of school property or, in this day, surrogate parents. The individuals and agencies appropriately assigned to address the various aspects of children's social and physical health, when they do their jobs, free teachers to be teachers. Freeing teachers to teach creates one of two, important, eventualities: 1.) Effective teachers will be even more effective, and 2.) Those incompetent teachers, who were using lack of support and cooperation as excuses for failure, will be exposed.

We do not take children to doctors' offices and ask physicians to act as surrogate parents. We do not ask museum curators to discipline our children as they visit exhibits. We do not expect restaurant owners to teach our children table manners. Nor do we look for amusement park ride operators to teach our children courtesy and respect for others in line. Let us not expect teachers to provide more social growth for our children, without our help, than academic growth, with our help. Teachers know that much social development comes with the territory. The question is, "Does the social development of children also come with parents?"

Few teachers join the profession for the pay. "Say, wha'?" Okay, *no* teachers join the profession for the pay. America must know, appreciate and acknowledge the fact that:

Our most dedicated civilian work force is our teachers!

They believe in our country. They believe in our children. They believe in themselves and their abilities to convince their students that:

Our most dedicated work force is our military heroes!

If, then, they can use the inspiration from this information as motivation for student participation in their own academic elevation, other PATS alliance partners will see the tangible fruits of their cooperation.

Following are *Seven Reasons Teachers Are Crucial to the Preservation of Our Nation:*

⇒ **Reason 1: Teachers affect the lives of more than 50 million children every day.**

According to the National Center for Education Statistics, "In Fall, 2013, about 50.1 million students will attend public elementary and secondary schools. An additional 5.2 million students are expected to attend private schools." [3]

In anticipation of the upcoming school year, the writers of this 2012 report informed America that our schools will, in 2013, impact the lives of millions of young people who hold our future in their hands. This is not a statement for lyrics to hopeful songs, nor the identification of an impressive market for advertisers (we hope). This population of children to teenagers subjecting themselves – that is, at parents' direction – to a particular set of supervisory adults, in similar numbers in 2014, is an undeniable demonstration of confidence in these adults' competence and morality.

Teachers' active daily influence (ADI, if it were a measurable phenomenon) on our children has the potential power to shape a revolution. Aren't we a Blessed nation to have such entrenched patriotic understandings and values that we do not worry that such a revolution is imminent? Our biggest worry, if you will, about America's schools is that they will not live up to our nationally understood and accepted intent to be the best in the world. Perhaps an American schools revolution is needed. We need 50-plus million American students to Declare Independence From Mediocrity. Let them assert a unified insistence that all Americans are endowed with the inalienable rights of lifelong learning and the pursuit of world leadership. Please do not take lightly the ability of school staff to maintain a patriotic student population of more than 50 million youth, year after year. Do not take lightly the strength of our nation to perpetuate this reality century after century.

⇒ **Reason 2: Your children spend an average of nearly 7 hours per day with teachers.**

"In most U.S. schools, the school day and year are the same length today as 100 years ago – 6 and1/2 hours, 180 days." [4]

45

The tenor of the sentence, above, seems to suggest that, perhaps, we need to increase the length of, both, the American school day and the American school year. To say that something is the same as it was 100 years ago might project a message of an inability or unwillingness to "keep up with the times."

The intent of this writing is to alert parents and other stakeholders to the significant reality of the amount of time classroom teachers spend molding and shaping the minds of American children. Perhaps we are not in school as long as foreign children are in school each day. Perhaps our school year is shorter. But, 180 days of 6.5 hours of engagement with 50 million impressionable minds gives educators of Pre-K through 12 students a lot of power. Select ten (10) parents at random. Ask each to write out, or type, their children's school schedules, including the names of their teachers with whom they are spending their time, and you might be disappointed to find out the number of American parents who have little, to no, idea what their children are doing, or with whom, while those children are in school.

I suspect that most all of us believe time spent in school is beneficial to our children, or they would not be sent, regularly, by willing parents and guardians to the campuses. But, there is a way to know for sure. Attend school with your children. In today's world, technology will make such visits possible when the in-person (preferable) encounter is not possible. For parents and guardians, frequent school visits may be inconvenient. The benefits of getting to know teachers and helping schools succeed far outweigh inconvenience. And, for those who think showing up at school, frequently, might be a bother to educators, let me tell you that your supportive presence is welcome. An administrative ally, Dr. Karen Williams, mentioned above, "showed up" in every classroom, everyday at Cordova Middle School. Teachers and students stayed "on their toes." What do you think might occur if parents and guardians "showed up" at school, once a week?

The school should be a welcoming place for everyone whose children are in attendance. Teachers should be a supported authority by everyone whose children are in attendance. More than six hours, per day, is a long time for young minds to be exposed to the personality, value system, knowledge, and teaching style of someone given the responsibility to help children grow. Articles of confirmation regarding the importance of teachers were published by 1.) Robert J. Marazano, Jana S. Marzano and Debra J. Pickering, who cited the work of S. Paul Wright, Sandra Horn and William Sanders and 2.) Brian Maienschein, who quoted Raj Chetty.

In their 2003 article, The Critical Role of Classroom Management, Marzano, Marzano and Pickering wrote the words, "We live in an era when research tells us that the teacher is probably the single most important factor affecting student achievement … " They cite research done on 60,000 students by Wright, Horn and Sanders who wrote: "The results of this study will document that the most important factor affecting student learning is the teacher." [5]

⇒ **Reason 3: No other single institution has this much responsibility for the stability of our nation's structure.**

Even as the Supreme Court functions to assure appropriate interpretation of the intentions of the United States Constitution,

Justices cannot appropriately interpret without having received the appropriate education.

The article, New Study Confirms the Importance of Teachers, by Brian Maienschein, contains the words of Raj Chetty, Harvard Economist who studied the academic achievement levels of 12,000 students : "…the most important factor was the quality of the teacher." [6]

You, citizens of The United States of America, are not entrusting your children into the hands – and influence – of impotent "baby-sitters," "child-sitters," "adolescent-sitters," "teen -sitters," "young adult-sitters." Those who hold in their hands the minds of our children hold the fate of our nation. Trust them. They mean us well and work hard to improve our plight. Join them. Your cooperation and assistance will improve their abilities to improve our plight.

While, at a high level of consciousness, American teachers may not arrive at school each morning thinking of the awesome responsibility they have to uphold the Constitution of The United States of America, or to maintain the ideological foundations of what makes us a free society that other nations seek to emulate around the world. But, American teachers are working, everyday, to make good citizens out of their students. The classroom teacher is not only "the most important factor" in determining the outcome of students' levels of achievement they are also the most important daytime factor in making students good American citizens.

School rules and codes of conduct help children become adults who follow laws and treat others with respect. Subject matter imparted in history and other social studies classes help students understand the foundations upon which we stand as we demonstrate what other nations envy. Socratic teaching engages student-teacher interaction in ways that help students consider not only from where we have come, but how we can improve upon our solid foundation as we seek to form "a more perfect union."

As a measure of time, the home and school share the greatest portions of students' days. Hopefully parents instill within their children a profound appreciation for living in the United States of America. What a privilege! Additionally, we would hope that parents guide their children in ways to make this great nation greater still for all American citizens. This is our hope for every household. For every school it is the charge. For teachers, it is their duty.

American schools are doing something right. America is, still, America. American schools must do something right now. We must make America better each day. Yes, the Supreme Court is crucial to our understanding how "rules" apply, as interpreted from the intent of those who wrote them. Indeed, American servicemen and women fight each day to protect us from enemies foreign and domestic. But, make no mistake. A child's understanding, and a teen's application, of codes of conduct that are consistent with what America stands for are in the job description of our teachers. Parents may instill this appreciation in their children. Teachers must instill this appreciation in their students.

⇒ **Reason 4: Teachers are monitors, and barometers of youth trends.**

Why would a sophisticated marching band from an A+ school appear in a nationally televised parade playing a very unsophisticated Hip-Hop hit? They would play the song because it's a hit. Some of the band members' dance moves may cause the school principal to wince a bit. But large numbers of young people, even from other schools, will show the utmost appreciation for the selection and some will dance right along with the featured band.

In this instance it's the band instructor who helps colleagues and parents to understand the culture that is today's youth. Other, similar, examples of teachers' awareness of how young people think and act collectively may come from the math teacher who uses rap music to aid students' memorization of facts or from the robotics club sponsor who helps members to build walking/rolling/interchangeable parts/speaking competitors or from geography teachers who take students on virtual trips to faraway places.

If the examples given, above, appear to be too academic, consider the informal school hallways which teachers govern nearly seven hours per day. Students travel back and forth between classes interacting with a comfort that reveals their "true" personalities (quotation marks "" added to suggest that even some young people's comfortable-appearing posture is contrived to impress peers). Alert teachers listen to and observe students who grow up in front of them without their realizing that they reveal, continuously, whom they seek to be, now. Some teachers must admit that some of the observing they do is as comfortable as students' hall behavior. In both cases their unintentional communication (students) and increased understanding (teachers) of students' personalities is as profound as – sometimes more profound than – any conscious mindset would have been.

One serious reason teachers must make professional assessments of student trends is related to safety and mental health. Students' behavioral trends may impact something as simple as a desire to be accepted (at times a more serious circumstance than at other times) or as deep as the formulation of suicide pacts. Teachers keep up with youth trends because they must in order to help parents and guardians keep them healthy and safe. Teachers keep up with youth trends because they can't avoid it – in the halls, in the cafeteria, in the openness and innocence of developing personalities.

This phenomenon has much broader implications than keeping up with young people's music and preventing suicide. The teacher-pupil relationship does not end with increasing achievement levels bolstered by instructors being able to identify with students' passions. American youth trends tend to bend towards wholesome ends. Even as parents didn't "get" Bo-Diddley, couldn't shake Elvis Pressley's shaking, were bugged by The Beatles, wanted Motown to keep making cars and stop making music and were convinced that for America rap "was a wrap," the great majority – the vast majority – of American adults from those eras are not just doing okay. They are leading their children to respect and maintain the character of the United States of America. Teachers are at the heart of that respect and maintenance. With all of the changes in slang and new names for different generations, respect for our nation is maintained by astute educators who can read student trends and then shape them into a consistent context of American pride. We must thank our educators for being able to teach the essence of being American to young people who don't always know that, in spite of trends, they're becoming better citizens.

⇒ **Reason 5: Teaching *is* the next step from parenting.**

"Parents are the child's first teacher." I don't know the source of the quote, but I know that those of us who repeat it sometimes act as though it is news. Some even begin the phrase with the word, "Actually".... While it is true that those of us who are, or have been, classroom teachers need to let parents know how much we respect their roles as guides to their children's learning well before they introduce them to a formal school setting, we should not act as though parents are unaware. We are speaking, here, of semantics not revelation. While parents do not share the job title, teacher, they certainly know that it is their role.

In like manner, asking teachers to serve as "surrogate parents" is an unnecessary request. Teachers are often – in fact, perhaps, definitely – the closest function to parenting children encounter day to day. As parents are expected to make good citizens of their children, teachers are expected to provide the consistent instruction that is complementary to parents' directions. One significant difference that distinguishes the guidance roles of teachers vs. parents is the fact that parents do not accept their responsibilities with a job description and mission statement. It is unfortunate that some parents – we would hope not many – can be irresponsible and, yet, be parents. An American teacher who is irresponsible in discharging the duties of guiding students cannot be a teacher. And, if one is found to be irresponsible with the position and authority of a real teacher should not be allowed in a teacher's place for long.

Keep in mind the amount of time spent by children and young adults in a place called "school", calculated above. Every minute of that time in an American school must reinforce the values that make us the country that we are and the developing nation we desire to be. Teachers cannot alter their job description, even for a little while, to accommodate personality dysfunction. We applaud parents who are "clean and sober" after going through programs that addressed their temporary setbacks from exemplary parenthood. Truly, it is remarkable when one can reform after confronting obstacles that might plague the best of us. But, even as the process may remove parents from their homes during rehabilitation, they are still parents. Any teacher confronting such, or similar, dysfunctions cannot continue to be called a teacher.

A parent taking parenting seriously is our fondest desire. A teacher serving as surrogate parent to your child must take teaching seriously as a requirement of serving, not as a fond desire. Mrs. Mattie Hopkins, a member of the Education Division of Operation PUSH said, in 1973, "Schools are the reproductive system of our nation." [7] This would suggest teachers' roles as parents go beyond their relationships with, and allegiance to, community residents with a stake in the local school. Teachers have the awesome responsibility of "parenting", if you will, the future of America. America is in good hands, or in jeopardy, depending upon the efficiency with which teachers grow the intellect and behavior of American students.

America must tolerate parenting challenges as we continue to improve upon services to help challenged parents. We hear too many stories of parents having to overcome violence, substance abuse, homelessness, illiteracy and more. This does not make all of them bad people. They need time to turn around their lives. America cannot tolerate dysfunctional teachers in classrooms. Being the closest relationship to parenting our children have, teachers must be ready to perform excellently at all times.

⇒ **Reason 6: Teachers define the role, regardless of the technology**

I suspect that my "lab table", with a sink and faucet, no less, the students and I used in room 214 in 1964 was the envy of pre-60's science teachers in Chicago's south side schools. We had a microscope students could take turns using, and the elemental chart that displayed the periodic table above the blackboard boasted 103 elements. (The periodic table is a table of the chemical elements in which the elements are arranged by order of atomic number in such a way that the periodic properties [(chemical periodicity)] of the elements are made clear.... On May 1, 2014, a paper published in Phys. Rev. Lett by J. Khuyagbaatar and others states the super heavy element with atomic number Z=117 (ununseptium) was produced...)[8]

America, please know that our teachers are staying abreast of advances in technology to assure that our children are up to date in, both, knowledge and application. While this may be the logical expectation, please understand that elementary and secondary schools, while creative and innovative, must react to the industries of technology, including our military, to determine what is appropriate (important, essential, crucial) to infuse in curricula and/or use in teaching. It is also the case that educators must keep up with inventors and marketers of frequently advancing technologies that are attractive for recreation and modern communication among our youth.

It is important that we consider the – yes, crucial – place teachers have always filled, and must always fill, from the "olden days" of all grades in one classroom that was the school, to futuristic virtual transplantable, "live", school experiences, worldwide, that do not require leaving the lab. The teachers' place is the fulfilling of the role of guiding learning in whatever setting is implemented or imposed. As we rush to top the technology of competitors far and wide, there will always be the need for efficient instruction from a well-prepared teacher. What is important to America – and, therefore, to the world – is that the race to the top must require a moral imperative. Regardless of the technology, American teachers are key to keeping learners on the path of using knowledge to create a better (more peaceful, more productive, healthier) world.

For centuries teachers have been depended upon to dispense fairness whenever conflicts arise. Even in today's world of cynicism and "viral" exposure of the failings of authoritative figures, including unfair teachers, the profession continues to be regarded as a knowledgeable source of justice and a fair arbiter of conflict. We continue to believe that teachers function for the well being of students and society. I suspect that one reason for confidence in America's teachers is their track record. There have been moments in time when major concern has been recorded over the delivery of excellence – or failure to deliver – in our schools (e.g., "A Nation At Risk" report, 1983).[9] America has registered decreasing confidence in our schools based upon comparisons to other countries. But, the concern is based upon the fact that we believe we are truly trying to deliver and in too many cases failing to do so. But American teachers' intentions to excel, and build strength of character within our borders has not been questioned. We have entered an era where near total transparency marks the advances in technology. However popular our music or strong our economy, the character of our country is determined by the consistency with which generations are taught who we are.

⇒ **Reason 7: Teachers teach.**

Teachers teach.

Measuring the impact of teachers' presence for the number of hours, per day, and number of school days, per year, they spend with America's youth is an artificial measurement if teachers are not engaged in teaching during those hours.

Teachers teach.

As helpful as the additional role of being observers, monitors and reporters of teen trends might be, it has little value if time and energy invested takes away from teaching.

Teachers teach.

As we place responsibilities in a patriotic context let us be mindful of the fact that there is nothing more patriotic than dedicated attention to the duty assigned after acceptance of the responsibility.

Teachers teach.

Surrogate parenting is a noble undertaking assumed almost "naturally" by those whose classrooms are welcome sanctuaries for children in need of stability, acceptance, care and – yes – love. But make no mistake. Teachers are not hired to raise other people's children. That welcome "parenting" climate must be in addition to, and not a substitute for, the professional work of teaching.

Teachers teach.

I love going to the barbershop. It is an age-old tradition of men gathering to catch up with friends, tell worn-out jokes and debate sports, politics, generational superiority and more. It would not surprise me to learn that a similar social atmosphere exists among ladies in beauty salons. But, whether we are in a hurry to get in and get out, or plan for time to linger, none of us intends to leave looking the way we looked when we arrived. To love the atmosphere does not address why I have come to the establishment. First, get me in the chair; *then* get me caught up on events. Children come to school to be taught. And while there are many legitimate strategies being used to enhance the classroom atmosphere, allowing children to attend school allowing teachers to leave without attending to their teaching is much worse than their parents going to barbershops and beauty salons then leaving without barbers or beauticians attending to their hair.

Teachers teach.

School administrators have allowed me to present a professional-development workshop with the title, *"Please leave teaching. Please leave, now. Don't wait. Don't hesitate. Don't pass go. Don't collect $200.00. Leave now, and succeed elsewhere."*

As harsh as the title might appear, I created it to make it very clear that I believe in the supreme importance of teaching. "Supreme importance" is not hyperbole. Teaching is a critical profession. To their credit, professional athletes and entertainers who command the international spotlight, to a person, talk about the profession of teaching being more important than what they, the athletes and entertainers, do for a living. I haven't seen any exceptions. Those of us who do not qualify, at 5'8" and 162 pounds, to play linebacker for a pro football team find ways to succeed in other fields with no sense of failure. If a person does not qualify to be a teacher, that person should feel comfortable seeking success in another field. Parents look to teachers to teach. Administrators expect teachers to teach. Students need teachers to teach. America demands that teachers teach. The future depends upon teachers teaching. Teachers insist that they want, desperately, to teach.

Teachers teach.

Chapter 4
S: **Students** As Patriotic Allies

The first three academic patriotism allies, **parents, administrators and teachers,** have unity of purpose: one all-important collective purpose. They work together for the social and academic growth of **students.**

Our American students must understand their importance to the preservation of our nation. For Real! Right Now!

The idea that our students are considered allies of American troops, as well as of parents, administrators and teachers, may be looked upon, by some, as a "cute" idea. Let's have them take photos with uniformed heroes and tell them that they are equally important. A few students just might take it seriously. A few military heroes just might consider the possibility. Someday, if we "play it" right, students may be seen as real patriots. Someday.

KNOW THIS! IT IS TRUE RIGHT NOW! WE CAN NO LONGER AFFORD TO WAIT UNTIL AMERICAN STUDENTS ARE FULLY CONVINCED OF THEIR IMPORTANCE BEFORE WE BEGIN TO TREAT THEM, ACCORDINGLY. I have heard Dr. Karen Young, when she was president of Learning 24/7, say that the wait is not necessary. During a presentation she made at an Effective Schools conference, I heard Dr. Young say something like, "We don't have to wait until children are believers to treat them like achievers." Her words were different, but the message that came through to me was children should be greeted then treated, immediately, as academic stars.

When I think about how soon, upon entering school, students should be informed of their importance and apprised of the school's high expectations, I think about recruits' welcome into our armed services. From my understanding of basic training in military service, those greeting recruits do not give them a week, or two, to become acclimated before treating them as full "partners" in their units. Imagine the following military scenario. What do you think?

PERHAPS, BECAUSE THEY ARE NEW TO THE ENVIRONMENT, YOUNG ARMED SERVICES RECRUITS SHOULD START THEIR BASIC TRAINING WITH THREE, OR FOUR, MORNINGS TO "SLEEP IN." THEIR LEADERS SHOULD LET THEM WEAR ATHLETIC JERSEYS BEARING HOMETOWN COLORS AND THE NUMBERS OF THEIR FAVORITE PLAYERS. CERTAINLY DRILL INSTRUCTORS SHOULD COMMAND AUTHORITY, BUT SHOULD NOT SPEAK TOO LOUDLY, SHOULD NOT USE CRUDE LANGUAGE, AND WHEN ASKED, SHOULD REPEAT COMMANDS SLOWLY AND SOFTLY SO THAT ALL WILL UNDERSTAND. DURING BASIC TRAINING THE DIFFERENT BRANCHES OF OUR ARMED SERVICES CAN INVITE OUTSIDE CONSULTANTS AND MOTIVATIONAL SPEAKERS TO COME IN AND CONDUCT TEAM-BUILDING EXERCISES INCLUDING WARM GET-ACQUAINTED "ICE BREAKERS" AND FUN BREAKOUT ACTIVITIES. THEN, THEY CAN GRADUALLY HELP SHAPE THE OUTFIT INTO A COHESIVE LOT WHO SING SONGS TOGETHER AFTER THEIR EVENING FAMILY

MEALS. THEN, BEFORE LONG, THEIR LEADERS SHOULD
BE ABLE TO CONVINCE MOST OF THEM OF THEIR
IMPORTANCE TO THE REST OF THEM AND, AFTER A
WHILE, THEY CAN FINALLY EXPLAIN THE OVERALL
MISSION OF THE GROUP. (Hmmm, maybe not.) Recruits are
greeted with the expectation of immediate conformity, not the
anticipation of gradual acculturation. The same attitude should
greet new, and returning, students.

Students need to know, immediately, upon entering school (in
fact, parents should inform them before they enter school), the
mission of the school and their importance as integral parts of that
mission. The students' role in the PATS (Parents, Administrators,
Teachers and Students) alliance must not be diminished because
of the students' youth. There is a Scriptural passage in the Holy
Bible that reads, *Let no man despise thy youth...*[10] The message
was sent from an older mentor to his young protégé. The intent
was to encourage the young man to use his gifts and wisdom to
lead others even when some others who were older resented the
assertion of leadership coming from someone so young. The
writer, the Apostle Paul, wrote to Timothy, a young leader, about
how to organize a church. We, older educators, mentors, and,
certainly, parents and guardians should write to our youth – and
speak to our youth – about how to organize their minds. They
must be convinced that though they are young, they are, yet,
important. Indeed, *because* they are young, they are *most*
important. Helping children to understand this role and
relationship must start at the earliest age of awareness. Children
should know that they are important, that they belong to an
important alliance and that they are expected to be highly

intelligent. Those are the marks of American students of all races, ethnicities, classes and even aptitudes.

One of the lesson titles in my Family Schooling manual is, *"Do Not Celebrate Your Child Doing Great."*[11] The suggestion, here, is to help our children to expect success. While congratulating good work is appropriate, we must not celebrate to the extent that it seems extraordinary. I created a title for a keynote address that was often requested (by very kind school administrators), probably, as much for the title as for its content. That title is, *"Nobody Rises To Low Expectations"*, and using same as the foundation for how I view teacher-pupil relations, my point was, and is, we must not be surprised when our children perform excellently. This is what they are supposed to do. Indeed, in the year, 2014, it is what American children must do. Excellent students are not only the end result of the strong alliance between American parents, administrators and teachers. American students are the central figures IN that alliance, participating as equal partners in creating, as well as being, the end result.

I suggest that we should not always celebrate children – American children – doing something great because to celebrate every time students do something great is to send the message that it is something exceptional. If American students are to be regarded as exceptional, they should be exceptional to other students around the world. To us, being excellent should be viewed as just "what, we are." To say that ranking more than ten places below other nations in international assessments of academic competencies is unacceptable is an unacceptable statement. American students lagging behind other nations is not just unacceptable, it is downright disrespectful to our fighting men and women who may be sent to "rescue" other nations whose children are more academically advanced than our own.

For students to function as equal partners in the PATS alliance, adults must empower them to assert that equality. Before children ever enroll in school, parents/guardians must teach them to regard this privilege, even at pre-school age, with patriotic anticipation. Children are America's most important citizens, as they are the guardians of our future. When administrators welcome families into the school family, they must help their new partners to embrace the school's belief system that spells out how our country depends upon our alliance working. Teachers in every classroom, everyday, must continually reinforce why teaching students is far more important than teaching subject matter. Teachers must communicate to students the message, "You (students) are the only reason all the rest of us are here. Your success is our principal mission. Our nation is depending on us. We will not allow you to allow us to let down our nation."

Academic Patriotism

Chapter 5
PATS: Proud to Be Allied With America's Armed Forces

The Parents, Administrators, Teachers and Students alliance is most certainly a natural alliance, as all seek to advance the intelligence of students that each succeeding generation will make our society – and, then our world - a better place to live. It is a natural alliance, to be sure. We should also be aware that the alliance between American school personnel and American military personnel is equally natural.

Though they should always be, there are times when PATS collectives are not regarded as "automatic" team members. However they are regarded, however smoothly, or disjointedly, they function, the alliance is always there, even when and where its' joint function needs to be improved. Our PATS must acknowledge this, and act accordingly, or our future is in peril. It should also be considered "automatic" for schools and military units to see themselves as, and functioning as, allies. If a member of an American military unit is asked what freedoms they protect in carrying out their duties, he, or she, may not say, specifically, "the right for American children and youth to have an excellent education", but, whatever freedoms are mentioned, they cannot be sustained and maintained without well taught citizens.

I cannot recall seeing a team of professional athletes being interviewed after winning a championship who failed to mention their fans in their expressions of appreciation. They always seem to talk about the fans as being an important part of the team (e.g., basketball references to "the sixth team member"). Upon mention of the fans, the remarks are met with loud cheers and demonstrations of significant enthusiasm – for a game! Soon, I hope that, both, service members, and students, will begin to speak with the same degree of respect and gratitude towards each other, as do athletes and fans. Certainly, military missions and academic accomplishments rise above the status of any game. This appeal to PATS and AAF is to ask that we acknowledge each other with the same degree of enthusiasm and gratitude, as do athletes and their fans towards each other. Successful missions should be followed with troop acknowledgements of the importance of students ("Their pursuit of excellence makes our resolve stronger"). Parents receiving praise for their children's academic accomplishments should be heard saying something to the effect: "Yes, we are proud, but we want our children to feel like it's the least we can do for those who make it possible for us to do it." Administrators acknowledging our rise upward several places in international testing results might utter the words, "We're moving in the right direction, as we continue to try to reach our military's level of global efficiency." Perhaps teachers seeing the strides being made by students now motivated by academic patriotism will be heard saying, "Our mission is tied to the mission of our military. We're just trying to keep up." And at least a million American students should now be heard saying, "Because of your sacrifice to defend our nation, I am serious about my education."

In a society that seems rife with cynicism and criticism, we are not surprised when various media generate capital by exposing human failure in its many forms. We appear to be especially intrigued and/or entertained by bringing to light the foibles and fables of public figures - the more public, the more vulnerable. Kudos to the news reporters and program producers who are proud to expose positive people and phenomena; who are proud to encourage audiences to support good programs featuring good people; who are proud to be American. Don't let the cynicism fool you. There is much to view that has socially redeeming qualities, and there are many American "fans" – too often overlooked – of civility, peace and patriotic progress.

Call me, "square." Academic Patriots, shaped by the unity of interacting allies must become at least as popular as athletes and entertainers. And, America can be proud of how many superstar athletes and entertainers agree. As opposed to creating something new, the "STOOTS for Boots" Campaign seeks to point out the myriad ways the PATS and Armed Forces alliances are working everyday. If you choose to become a part of this campaign in a way that this book recommends, or if you will let us show other ways you complement us, thank you. The main thing is for us to help each other convince all others that there is a "natural alliance" that exists between American parents, administrators, teachers, students, *and* servicemen and women that needs strengthening and sustaining.

Chapter 6
If You Can't Fight, Don't Join 'Em

Perhaps you are not a parent, administrator, teacher or student. This does not mean, for a moment, that you cannot be a member of the team that this alliance represents. Their alliance is natural based upon the fact that, by definition, they are united to advance the safety, instruction, intelligence, and health - as well as the academic and social maturation - of our children. Then, considering our American military heroes a "natural" addition to this alliance is not a stretch when we contemplate why they make the sacrifices – including the ultimate sacrifice – they make for our country. If our children are not taught why, and how, to preserve the freedoms for which warriors fight, those warriors' sacrifices are, then, made in vain. You, too, can join the alliance without having the title of any of the above. But, "If you can't fight, don't join 'em."

Your name does not have to be Acey to be a fighter. (When I grew up in the 1950s on the south side of Chicago, Acey Harris was the toughest brother in the Ida B. Wells housing projects.) As did the great Muhammad Ali, Acey defeated most opponents in their minds before the physical fight began. Later in life, it was the mental engagements that were most formidable in Acey's fighting experiences. After becoming one of the nicest adults anywhere, Acey Harris has found himself trying to capture, and in most cases trying to change, the minds of young men who wanted to fight the way he used to. He tries to convince young people that there is more to fighting than physical confrontations, and that many non-physical fights require greater toughness than the physical. Among such confrontations are the current day wars for our children's minds and talents. They need your help. But, if you can't fight, don't join 'em.

American adults must answer the following question, individually and collectively: "Are our children worth fighting for?"

Does this read like a rhetorical question? I hope so. We should be able to take it for granted that the answer is an obvious, "Yes!"

Let me begin this particular thought by explaining what I mean by "fight" within the topical context here. I am suggesting that a worthy fight for American children is not limited to, but includes:

- Defending our children against harmful human beings, objects and substances;

- Teaching our children how to identify what is good for them, and how to apply what is good to their personal growth and social interactions;

- Advocating on behalf of our children without fear of reprimanding our children;

- Keeping up with our children's progress in school for as long as they're in school;

- Assuring that our children present their "best selves" to the world, including their best communication skills and appropriate attire;

- Speaking for our children when their "argument" is with adults; and disciplining our children when they try to argue with adults; and,

- Making our children's world – local and global – safe, peaceful and happy.

If a document so lofty as the Declaration of Independence can include "the pursuit of happiness" as a chief tenet of America's promise to her citizens, certainly mentors, coaches, employers, sponsors, organization leaders, and all others who serve to protect children's childhood, joining the alliance, can make that pursuit a chief element in our fight to help the youth stay young long enough to become well-adjusted adults. We have known for a few decades that the fight for our children's minds is one that is formidable. Today's technology finds us having to look around phones and look over (but, not overlook) tablets and other social media equipment and apparatuses to engage young folks' attention. But, the objects are far less problematic than the content.

American adults who are not parents, administrators and/or other formal members of the school alliance are, still, stakeholders. This means, simply, that we all have a stake in the outcomes of our students' performances in school. If they do well in school, it bodes well for America's future. If American students fail to take school seriously, they will fail seriously in school. As courageously as our military makes sacrifices, and as devotedly as our school alliances address academic excellence, they need all stakeholders to join them. However, if you can't fight, don't join 'em. Amendment: If you choose not to fight, you have already chosen not to join them.

Among the challenges this campaign puts forward to students is projected in the form of the question: "Can you look into the eyes of a military hero, and justify 'playing around' in school?" I ask stakeholders a similar question: "Can you claim that you are not a part of the alliance that functions to guard your future?" It has been said, often, "If you are not a part of the solution, you are a part of the problem." I suggest that, "If you are not a part of the solution, you *are* the problem." If you are not a part of the solution, you are apart from the solution, and your country needs your serious assistance in honoring our troops by helping American students excel.

There are things you can do in the fight to expose and exploit the greatness our children possess potentially and currently. You may consider the bullet-point list, above, that speaks to defending, teaching, disciplining and more. Additionally, you may look for organizations working with young people to join or to assist as volunteers. This affiliation is not only productive but also protective. In, both, formal and informal settings, please share personal stories that are instructional, inspirational, and pertinent to "the American dream" that our armed forces are fighting to protect. Your fight for our children's minds to develop an appreciation for patriotism is no less noble, and, from a psychosocial perspective, is in many ways more formidable. Our children are worth the battle. They must be taught the worth of those in battle. Please join America's parents, administrators, teachers, students, servicemen and women, veterans and fellow stakeholders. Please be a part – an equal part – of the solution. But, if you cannot fight …..

Defining the fight determines the weapons.

Being engaged in "a battle for our children's minds" demands weapons of patience, understanding, presence and informed authority. These weapons must be used, not only by parents and teachers but, also, by all adults who make up "the village" responsible for raising the child. In her article, *Understanding Youth Popular Culture (YPC) And The Hip-Hop Influence,*[12] Patricia Thandi Hicks Harper, Ph.D., writes:

Despite adult attitudes (positive and negative) about youth culture, we know we must have a working knowledge of this culture that engulfs and contextualizes our young people's lives if we are to effectively communicate with them. It is important to understand the information that they process. The rules of social marketing are pertinent and suggest that effective communication begins with knowing your target audience. Collectively, youth in America represent a powerful movement that transcends race, ethnicity, gender, and social or economic status. America's youth are a walking depiction of their worldview that is externally manifested through clothing, art, attitude, style, movement, music, video, television, film, language and the World Wide Web.

Later, she writes:

Many of America's youth need Adult assistance, nurturing, supervision, and resources because they are at risk for making negative and harmful behavioral choices. Those entities that will succeed in reaching these young people with their messages .... are those who are the most culturally competent in youth popular culture and who use this knowledge and experience as a foundation for their education and information dissemination outreach strategies.[13]

The words, "...those who are the most culturally competent", may refer, directly, to you. While there may be an expectation that those who understand children best are those who have children, the reality is, often, quite different. Many citizens without their own children have been called Mom and Dad more than some adults with children. It may, certainly, be a fact that, because the time spent with young people by those with no parental responsibilities is easier time to spend; but, for whatever reason, there are myriad relationships where non-alliance alliance members can be most helpful. Your cultural competency may result from having the time to be dispassionately engaged in learning "all about" America's youth. Your value to our American alliance of adult caretakers of our youth can be derived from your appearing to show extra care because (theoretically) "you don't have to get too personally involved."

The undeniable fact is that you – that we all – can rest assured (though, assuredly, we cannot rest) that there are no small adult roles in the task of teaching our children that they owe our military respect and equal effort to preserve our nation's future. There can be no fun in entering foreign territory, avoiding explosive hidden mines, with hostile forces seeking to foil our every attempt to calm the threats of dangerous, even suicidal, acts by even small children – especially, when that "foreign territory" is an American neighborhood and the hidden mines are, actually, "hidden minds."

Dr. Thandi Hicks Harper is not alone in her assessment of the popularity – thus, the power – of the personalities of American youth. Our Hip-Hop culture, in particular, has captured the imaginations of youth – and, for that matter, adults – around the world.

In an article written for the Journal of Urban Youth Culture, titled, *Hip-Hop and Youth Culture* by Carl S. Taylor, Ph.D. and Virgil Taylor, in its updated, May 1, 2014 form the following observation was made:

Hip-Hop, once limited to urban music and dance has become a widespread form of communication exhibited and enjoyed by young people throughout the world. Hip-Hop is no longer limited to rap music and break dancing; today it represents a multi-billion dollar industry that influences everything from automotive design and fashion to prime-time television programming, collegiate and professional sports, mass media marketing and Madison Avenue advertising. Today Hip-Hop is for many a way of life, a culture that is intricately woven into every aspect of young people's daily lives.

..... Hip-Hop was initially born of the ability of those early practitioners of rap music, DJ wizardry and street-corner fashion creation to overcome their inability to gain acceptance and recognition by the established music, fashion and entertainment industries.

Further galvanizing the fledgling culture was the lack of acceptance by the adult culture, who refused to recognize these emerging forms of expression as legitimate. This was particularly true where many parents were concerned. Needless to say, if parents and other authority figures didn't understand Hip-Hop, didn't like it and, in many instances, admonished young people for embracing it, young people were even more compelled to further immerse themselves in the newly developing culture.[14]

Let us, please, keep in mind that "Hip-Hoppers" attend our schools. It is important that they be taken seriously as integral members of our PATS alliance. As a sub-culture, if referred to by the nomenclature, Hip-Hop, these young people become the stereotypical antithesis of patriotism, oftentimes, unfairly. Again, while admitting that I did not have the honor of serving in America's military, I can well imagine that new recruits are stripped of their Hip-Hop personalities rather quickly, upon arriving for duty. However, while they are American students, if we refrain from stereotyping them – or any group – and appeal to their intelligence and sense of team spirit, they may just offer listening ears and open hearts to respecting those who fight for them.

Hip-Hop has been with us for more than three decades. The "parents" who once "admonished young people for embracing" Hip-Hop are grandparents. The Hip-Hop young people who were "admonished" are, now, parents themselves. This is a good thing. Not only do they understand the culture, and embrace it, but their examples of success and sobriety show us that these young people have the same potential as those who had Elvis Pressley and the Beatles "to overcome their (1950s and 1960s) inability to gain acceptance and recognition by the established music, fashion and entertainment industries." What's more, it is my steadfast belief – part of my overall belief system – that, given the right motivation, this community of young people will rise to the heights of American academic achievement to the envy of students the world over. If you want to see some authentic excitement, watch what happens when American students, from "Hip-Hoppers" to other non-stoppers, emerge on top of all nations, in every academic category, because all of **our** respect for **our** military heroes caused **our** students to choose to excel!

Yes, weapons of patience, understanding, and expressions of agape, unconditional, love for young people longing to be accepted, are appropriate in a fight that is defined by adults as a confrontation to win the hearts and minds of America's youth. Let us keep our hearts and minds open to the reality of their struggle to win us over, as well. They are reaching out to us though they (and we) are unaware of their reaching. Sometimes we must fight our inner selves to attract their better selves. We must fight against our own prejudices as they relate to stereotypes about youth that we pretend were never visited upon us. Today, we need our young people to be sober, intelligent, united and patriotic more than ever. Our world grows smaller with every technological innovation. Our opponents grow more formidable with every young American genius we lose to self-destructive behavior, or is rendered irrelevant by intellectual forfeiture due to drugs, misplaced peer pressure and/or refusal to study. We are engaged in the kind of domestic warfare with our youth that causes us to neglect our true heroes who are engaged in justifiable, real, battles in distant lands – for us. Our young people need us to be with them as they grow. They need us to be living examples of respect for true heroes. They need us to fight for their patriotic possibilities, academic and civic. But, if you can't fight (using the appropriate weaponry), don't (try to) join 'em.

CONCLUSION

I was not very tough when I grew up. Acey was tough. I was reasonably popular because I was something of a comedian. My sense of humor kept me out of a lot of fights. But, I did learn that all fights were not about physical toughness. I grew to admire classmates, who "fought" – the midnight oil, unreasonable professors and high tuition – to get through college. I saw Civil

Rights leaders "fight" on their knees, in prayer for their attackers. I continue to see parents "fight" to keep their children safe, sober and successful. I am a citizen of a nation whose "fight" to preserve our liberties and lifestyle is often political, economical and ideological rather than always physical.

Children will never know what a true fight is if they only see physical confrontations in local locations with no explanation – beyond reputation – for the altercations. We must do more to define fighting than, simply, discussing what it is and/or what it should be. By example, we must demonstrate that our children are important enough to fight for. By word, and by example, we must help our children to understand that our fight for them is our domestic responsibility to show our military fighters that we respect and appreciate their "real" fights for our nation.

If we have no children in school, nor any family members in our armed forces, we do not have a "legal" obligation to join the academic patriotism campaign. But, if we agree that those in the military protect us whether, or not, we have school-aged children; and, if we agree that all of our future depends upon children in school, we should, then, agree that we have as great a responsibility to join this fight as any other American citizens. The chapter title, "If you can't fight, don't join 'em", suggests that it is better that you remain on the sidelines of destiny than to be counterproductive with uninformed activism. The most sophisticated weapons trained upon friends are more destructive than being uninvolved. But, knowing that you are needed – and, you are – to fight besides your fellow American citizens for a partnership between students and troops, should cause you to want to learn what you can do, then, to learn it, and to do it. If you can't fight, don't join. But, I guarantee that you can fight, and you are sorely needed.

Academic Patriotism

Chapter 7
More Than A Pledge, A Promise
("With Respect for the Field on the Shield")

"**Because of your sacrifice to defend our nation, I am serious about my education.**" Twenty-eight (28) students offered this statement of commitment at a press conference held at their school – Ruskin Senior High School, Kansas City, Missouri – on May 15, 2014. The school's JROTC Drill Instructor, Colonel Ivan Glasco (USMC Retired), arranged for each of the students to select a veteran from among the special military guests present. Each student then recited the pledge, directly, to that person. The press conference was shown on local TV news outlets, and announced on local radio stations. It was a "feel good" event, all around.

The question that was never asked by any of the reporters covering the ceremony was, "How do we know you (the students) are serious?" Some of the students made statements, later, expressing a desire to keep in touch with the veterans. Likewise, the veterans expressed the same interest in the other direction. The sincerity of the pledge will be proven in the efforts the students make in class, and in their keeping in touch with (interacting with) the veterans.

When someone noticed that Colonel Glasco had written, "USMC Retired", on a document, they asked, "Oh, you were a Marine?" Colonel Glasco was quick to respond, "I am retired, but

I'll always be a Marine." Now, that's commitment. That is being serious. That is making - and keeping - a promise.

One of the great student benefits to be derived from a relationship with American warriors is that of seeing what disciplined commitment acts like at a professional and patriotic level. Students in an extracurricular school club, or on a school team, can play around if they want. If it costs the club its reputation, or causes the team to lose in competition, it is quite likely that many people will be upset. The students' conduct will probably cost them their memberships in the club or on the team. A warrior in battle does not "play around" because such conduct will exact the high cost of lives, including that of the person guilty of the offense.

One reason we do not see such behavior in America's military is because the consequences of such foolishness are realized very quickly, and very publicly. It is important for America's students to know and understand the ultimate consequences of their actions in school. While not seen very publicly or considered immediately, the impact of American students' academic mediocrity on the very lives of fellow Americans, at home and abroad, is real, long lasting and, therefore, a clear and future danger to our country's leadership in the world.

Let us look at some comparative data: An article that appeared in the Economist, January 19, 2012 posted a list that ranked countries "educationally." They included:

Finland

South Korea

Hong Kong

Japan

Singapore

Britain

Netherlands

New Zealand

Switzerland

Canada

Denmark

Australia

Poland

Germany

United States

(Names at ranks 11 and 16 were omitted)

The article stated that there were many international reports on educational comparisons. "Now a newcomer is trying to dig deeper. 'The Learning Curve' is published by Pearson (our – the Economist's – part owner) and compiled by the Economist Intelligence Unit (the Economist's sister company). It uses the existing measures, but adds criteria such as graduation rates, adult literacy and the effects of years in school on productivity.

"This method does not change the picture at the top: Finland, South Korea and Hong Kong shine as usual, followed by Japan and Singapore. But other changes are sharp. Britain gained sixth place, whereas in the PISA (Programme for International Student Assessment) 2011 report England (without Scotland and Wales) came 25th in reading and 28th in maths." [15]

An Internet website, YO Expert Pro Writers. Pro Answers, fielded the question: "How do United States students compare to students in other countries?"

The question was answered by *Marian Wilde,* an expert in the *Matters in Education,* category. *Marian* responded:

"It's not as bad as some say, but there is room for improvement. The United States may be a superpower but in education we lag behind. In a recent comparison of academic performance in 57 countries, students in Finland came out on top overall... Other top-performing countries were: Hong Kong, Canada, Taiwan, Estonia, Japan and Korea.

"How did the U.S. do? Students in the United States performed in the middle of the pack. On average, 16 other industrialized countries scored above the United States in science and 23 scored above us in math. Experts noticed that the United States' scores remained about the same in math between 2003 and 2006... Meanwhile, many other nations, Estonia and Poland being two, improved their scores and moved past the U.S." [16]

An Executive Summary from the Economic Policy Institute reported that, "In December, 2012, the International Association for the Evaluation of Educational Achievement (IEA) released national average results from the 2011 administration of the Trends in International Mathematics and Science Study (TIMSS). U.S. Secretary of Education, Arne Duncan, promptly issued a press release calling the results "unacceptable" saying that they "underscore the urgency of accelerating achievement in secondary school and the need to close large and persistent achievement gaps" ..." [17]

And, a report in Education Week, July 18, 2014 cited a statement from President Barack Obama, made in 2011. The quote from the article: "It is an undeniable fact that countries who out-educate us today are going to out-compete us tomorrow," the President declared at a White House event in September (2011).

"If we are serious about building an economy that lasts – an economy in which hard work pays off with the opportunity for solid middle-class jobs – we've got to get serious about education." [18]

Lives are affected by what American students do, or fail to do, in school. President Obama called for "seriousness" well before the May 15, 2014 pronouncement of our very sincere Ruskin High students. Dedicated American teachers were calling for seriousness before the President's pronouncement. Dedicated American teachers were calling for seriousness not only before I began making the appeal, but, well before I began my teaching career in 1964. You want young people to know their real/authentic importance just as military leaders want their troops to understand. The impact of student conduct may not be as sudden as what happens on the battlefield, but the consequences can be as devastating and, in many cases, have a much longer-lasting impact on the stability of our nation. Students, please remember, "Your nation needs you."

"With Respect for the Field on the Shield"

A young lady, Cristina Shell is a Graphic Illustrator for a Kansas City radio broadcasting company, The Carter Broadcasting Group. She was very patient with me as I described what I'd like to have as a logo for the "STOOTS for Boots" Campaign. Her initial renderings were outstanding. I wanted to add the slogan, "Your Boots, Our Books" to let all who view the logo see that the boots and the books go together in a dynamic way. The final drawing, with which I am more than pleased, features Stars and Stripes surrounding the Boots and Books drawn on a silver shield. This logo will be seen on lapel pins, T-Shirts, caps, bumper stickers, etc.

As this chapter seeks to motivate American students to become more serious about their academic pursuits, one can easily see the desirability of our students taking lessons from America's military. Our men and women in uniform display insignia and emblems that identify their branches of service, and pertinent data about their ranks, placements and accomplishments in their various units and assignments. Whether an emblem denoting branch of service or special unit, or an insignia indicating rank, I have never seen a man or woman in the military allow anyone to show disrespect for what he, or she, is wearing. More importantly, I am pleased (and proud, having never served, myself) when I see members of the United States Armed Services who refuse to show disrespect, themselves, for what they are wearing.

The silver shield upon which rests the "STOOTS for Boots" logo is designed to be worn as a lapel pin, a patch on a blazer or sweatshirt, on a cap, or in some other fashion.. We would love to see millions of American students wear The Field (the Stars of the Stars And Stripes) on the Shield. What a great display for an effort that seeks to encourage students across the country to take seriously their responsibility for preserving our nation's future. However, if the displaying of the logo is only to advertise this campaign, it defeats the fundamental purpose of the campaign. It would be better to see fewer pins on very serious students than to see many pins on less serious students wearing them only until the cameras stop rolling.

"With Respect for the Field on the Shield" is a caption that does not appear on the logo, itself. The "STOOTS for Boots" Campaign hopes that this shield will be worn with a profound respect, and pride, emblazoned on the wearers' *hearts*.

Worthiness to wear the symbol does not demand earning the highest academic grades, except for those who could were it not for a non-caring attitude. Please wear "The Field on The Shield" if you are a dropout who decided to drop in again, out of respect for our military. Please wear "The Field on The Shield" if you've been a chronic absentee who is, now, making every effort to attend class regularly, on time, because you honestly believe that American military service personnel deserve your best. Wear "The Field on The Shield" if you are courageous enough to leave a street gang that carries weapons to hurt or kill others on American streets because you finally realize that those who carry weapons on foreign battlefields need leaders like you to stay healthy. They need you to welcome them home to neighborhoods that are safer than where they had to fight to keep you and your rival gang members alive. Please wear "The Field on The Shield" if you believe that you can be as serious about school as students in Finland, South Korea, Hong Kong and Japan! And, yes, please wear "The Field on The Shield" if you are an excellent student. You are the model of what the campaign seeks to project.

Perhaps some students have not, yet, noticed that the term "nerd" does not have the stigma it had a few decades ago. While some sitcoms and movies make fun of the term, our high tech society makes it plain that "nerds" are in demand for their creative intelligence and high (tech) aptitudes in related fields.

Unfortunately, there are still some students who are concerned about the peer pressure that is attached to being "too academic." There's no stigma attached to being too "hip" (hop). There is no stigma attached to being too athletic. There is no stigma attached to making too many people laugh at other people. But, if any of the hip, athletic, comedic popular students ever "make it big", they need to realize that it will be nerds signing their checks.

The "STOOTS for Boots" Campaign wants to thank you in advance of your wearing the symbol. We know that you are good. That's not what the "Thank you" is for. We thank you for knowing that you are good, yourself, and for having the maturity to make the statement ("Because of your sacrifice to defend our nation, I am serious about my education.") for all to see. We thank you for letting your example shine in front of your fellow students. Please know that we know you do not have to wear this campaign's pin, T-shirt, cap or blazer. You can show America's military that you respect them by telling those with whom you have contact of your intention to "get serious" for them; and, then, doing it. "With Respect For..." is not reserved for the field on the shield. It means showing respect for your country and the warriors who keep us safe.

Let's get serious. Our enemies are already !

Begging forgiveness for the awkward "common" reference to "already are," please know that the spirit of the phrase is more important than the grammar.

"Our enemies *are* already" seeking to best America in many facets of world leadership, and their serious focus on education should cause us to consider the comparisons, above. All enemies do not bear arms. All enemies are not political and/or ideological.

The free online dictionary, Dictionary.com defines the word, enemy, among other, harsher definitions, as, an adversary or opponent. America has many opponents; even, in some cases, "friendly opponents", who are open competitors in markets that require broad knowledge and high intelligence.

While the countries listed above the United States in the surveys discussed, above, do not constitute "a list of enemies", they do constitute a list of competitors. Others who declare themselves, openly, as enemies are certainly seeking to outsmart us. American students must not allow academic superiority to be an easy acquisition for adversaries based upon casual attitudes towards education. I could have used a "softer" term such as adversary or opponent in my subtitle, above. However, it is time for America to treat the matter of student preparation for world leadership as a patriotic priority rather than a national (Americans vs. Americans) competition. Even if we are "bested" in technology, indigenous production, economics and/or creative entrepreneurship by a "friendly" competitor, our nation will be subject to dependency on another nation's (other nations') agenda (s). We must take this matter seriously.

The United States of America cannot afford to see fellow citizens as more threatening opponents than those who would deny the rights of fellow citizens to disagree. From political opponents to athletic fans; from rival gangs to diverse racial/ ethnic groups; from business rivals to, even, differing faiths, Americans can become such fierce adversaries that coexistence seems impossible, in some instances, right here in our own common country – which happens to be, to the envy of many around the world – a very uncommon country, deserving of our united protection.

We can ill afford to let genius go to waste because it might give my political opponent an edge if I openly agree that it is genius. Heroes facing real foreign foes deserve better from our leaders.

Athletic fans willing to actually fight each other over differing opinions about who's best should feel foolish whenever they stand, as one, for the singing of our National Anthem. Our fighting men and women love a good game as much as the rest of us; but, there's no justice in them having to see a "good fight" among friends at home when they have just returned from a bad fight overseas against enemies.

Rival gangs brandishing weapons – as stated before – should learn from America's military heroes the authentic reasons for using lethal force. Those who sacrifice, abroad, to protect American streets should never have to see blood in them when they return home.

American cultural diversity should yield to the cultural commonality that molds the majestic multicultural mosaic that makes America magnificent. American servicemen and women do not limit their protection of fellow warriors only to those who are from the same race or socioeconomic backgrounds. They must return home to students from every demographic displaying the same seriousness and excellence across the sociological spectrum.

American businesses hungry to top other businesses must make keeping all Americans from being hungry a top priority. When veterans are seen carrying signs in the street it is a sign that the rest of us are guilty of negligence.

About differing faiths, I wrote the following, using the title, Buddha Cried, "Please Do":

When I came shouting, "Praise The Lord,"

Buddha Cried, "Please Do."

Allah smiled, and Yahwe said, "We praise in our ways, too."

"As-Salaam-Alaikum" "Peace" "Shalom."

"Nam-Myoho-Renge-Kyo"

You love One God, or Witness Two.

I believe in The Holy Trio.

You're not required to believe as I,

but I am required to love you.

Your faith is different, I know not why,

but God knows I am not above you.

Our Natives honor Mother Earth:

The Land; The Sky; The Water.

"We all are one" the great tribes say;

and, so says God, The Father.

What teach we, now, the child unborn,

innocent 'til taught different;

That other faiths are ours to scorn?

Are we, now, God's equiv'lent?

Or, do we teach in word, and deed,

based on the faiths we chose,

That all are children of One Seed,

Whatever cloth their clothes?

So, when I come shouting,

"Praise the Lord," and Buddha cries, "Please do."

The world is then on one accord when I show my love for you.

In America, I can write this, I can recite this. I can be a born-again Christian - and, I am – and, I respect the rights of other Americans to practice other faiths. I can do this because someone in an American uniform protects our rights to worship, or not to worship, and yet enjoy full participation in the benefits of American citizenship. If there are foes seeking to destroy what makes us "the land of the free, and the home of the brave", by teaching their children more efficiently than we teach our own, it is past time for us to become as serious as they; indeed, even, more-so, as we have more to lose should we allow ourselves to be outsmarted.

CONCLUSION

America has great teenagers. To the degree that their brain development allows them to mature, they are remarkably loyal to the mores of our society, even as they "test" the parameters of legality and civility, as did we (I'm, now, 72) at their age. Adhering to what makes America the envy of other nations does not require perfect conduct. Find me a perfect 14-year old and I'll run for cover from whatever is about to strike. But, even miscreants define their misbehavior based upon defying American norms that include politeness, civil language, fair play, obedience, honesty, respect – especially for elders and rules of law – sobriety and other traits that keep us safe and strong. It is difficult to be anti-social without having an appreciation for what being social means.

Since teens are the idols of children and the hope of elders, their patriotism, whether or not they admit to it, has stabilized America for centuries. We must believe in them. We must trust that they have the discipline and maturity to make promises and to keep them. Because they are teens (remember?), we who teach them, mentor them and, most of all, who parent them must accompany our trust with guidance and consistent presence. Stable families tend to be able families. Teens often make promises with the greatest intentions of keeping them. The personal confusion that comes with growing up plus peer influence towards rebellion can keep some promises from being kept. Many adult promises suffer a similar fate, sometimes for the same, or very similar, reasons.

But coach Bush, and choir director Stevenson, and robotics club sponsor Wells will show us what happens when teenage, and younger, students engage membership in an activity that "captures their whole hearts." Promises made to stay on the team, sing in the choir or participate in a STEAM fair are promises that are kept for two compelling reasons: passion and guidance. Young people who feel strongly about being a part of (belonging to) an activity that they "own", and that allows them to "shine", guided by a "hands on", consistent, mentor is likely to keep them engaged for as long as the passion and guidance remain. Add positive publicity to the equation and the passion, being reinforced, will grow.

American students, including young students influenced by teens, can make a pledge become a promise when ignited by passion for being what (being those who) make America great. Stimulating the passion is the guidance – by distant example and personal contact – of uniformed coaches, choir directors and club sponsors "all rolled up into one" heroic military team of world leadership. American students *will* turn a pledge into a promise when they are made to realize their authentic importance to our nation's very survival as the highest representation of "liberty for all" that history has ever witnessed. It may not be fair that this awesome responsibility is visited upon their innocent youth; but, if we are to maintain our status, our students must pledge, promise and prove their true excellence.

Book 2:
The Proof

Proud PATS in Action

Insuring Domestic Responsibility

Insuring Domestic Responsibility

Parents, Teachers, Administrators, Students and American Armed Services personnel are forever allied in accepting joint responsibility for securing our nation: our safety, our intellectual productivity, our progress, our moral compass ever pointed towards magnets of "life, liberty and the pursuit of happiness." [19]

Those who agree with the premise of Book 1, that the alliance connecting home, school, the military and stakeholders impacted by academic achievement must work together may wonder how. Book 2, *Proud PATS in Action,* gives America's schools ideas and examples to consider emulating as you seek to carry out your patriotic responsibilities. America is fortunate to have enough models to follow that all schools can succeed when all school allies work in unity.

The Preamble to the Constitution of the United States of America includes the words, "...insure domestic tranquility" [20] While appreciative of its lofty intent, we have seen times in the United States when we have not been "domestically tranquil." We have seen unrest and violence in our history. We must applaud the efforts of all who work for justice, peace, unity and tranquility in this nation. But, to insure tranquility is, sometimes, an elusive quest. We can, however, insure domestic responsibility. That is, each of us can insure that we will be responsible citizens in the effort to maintain America's leadership in the world.

"Insuring Domestic Responsibility", as I am using the phrase here, refers to a commitment we can make as individuals coming together to make our nation a better place to live for all. One thing that should unify us all is respect for our American men and women in uniform. One delivery system we can use to

demonstrate our collective respect is America's schools. This Book (2) will show that all systems are not the same, but you have read that the two entities required to define a place called school are students and teachers. Many different strategies are used to support, and achieve, success in different schools; but all American schools are unified in our aim to be the best in the world. It is the belief of this campaign that universal agreement on the patriotic incentive to perform can enhance the achievement levels of American students across the country. We can insure that we shall take (domestic) responsibility for our various roles in improving schools in need of improvement, and supporting schools that are already exemplary.

The "STOOTS for Boots" Campaign seeks to share what effective schools are doing to be effective. We begin with what effective schools have done through the courtesy of the producers of a video series they did in 1998. The outline of our STOOTS' twelve-step approach to achieving excellence looks back to the featured examples from the video series to highlight the twelve progressive concepts. These brief written summaries of their programs are covered in full in the video, which we have permission, through **Teachscape** (San Francisco) to use in professional development presentations.

Chapter 8
Excellence Is a Choice

"If you follow the 3 basic steps as outlined in this book exactly and don't earn straight A's, we will give you one hundred dollars!"

This guarantee is not just a statement. It follows the title of Donna O. Johnson's and Y.C. Chen's book, *Guaranteed 4.0* – A simple 3-step brain-based learning system to help students learn how to learn.[21] As helpful as this book is to college and university students, so is their book, *Guaranteed A+ plus*,[22] helpful to high school students; and it offers the same $100 guarantee.

Obviously, the guarantee, the books, and the workshop are not about the money. They are about students deciding – making the **choice** – to excel and, then following through.

"No, every one of us is smart."

In his book, *Outliers The Story of Success* [23], Malcolm Gladwell tells the story of a young girl, Marita, who attended the Bronx KIPP Academy, when she was twelve years old. Pointing out that her plight – living in a one- bedroom apartment with a single mom, free lunch recipient, low socio-economic surroundings, – would, ordinarily, be seen as a predictor of being on the low end of the "achievement gap", Gladwell reports that her success, and the success of others like her, depends upon time on task. Her, **"everyone of us is smart"**, statement was made to a friend who was complimenting her on how smart she was to do so well at KIPP. Marita was saying it was an investment in intellectual discipline and time that was a part of the KIPP philosophy, and practice, for all of their students.

Citing a 1990s study, conducted by psychologist, K. Anders Ericsson and two colleagues, and a quote from neurologist, Daniel Levitin, about the study, Malcolm Gladwell writes, "The emerging picture from such studies is that ten thousand hours of practice is required to achieve the level of mastery associated with being a world-class expert – in anything."[24] Levitin goes on to say, "In study after study, of composers, basketball players, fiction writers, ice skaters, concert pianists, chess players, master criminals, and what have you, this number comes up again, and again…."

Yes, Marita, "…**every one of us is smart**" when we are smart enough to **choose** study time, discipline, a sense of purpose and hours of practice over wasting time and brain power.

"Tell the '24/7' story."

My wife, of 27 years, "Wonderful Wanda" Boyd, indulges my storytelling, though she has heard many of them several – even, many – times. One of the stories I have repeated in lay sermons at many Christian churches speaks to the subject at hand.

Before moving from Chicago, Illinois to Kansas City, Missouri in February, 1980,

I spent five months, from mid-September, 1979 until February 18, 1980 managing the night shift at a south side establishment that, by then, had seen much better days. I was honored to work for the gentleman who owned this establishment, as I had/have the utmost respect for him. But, by this time, after many years of "neighborhood transition", my chief responsibility was to engage pimps, prostitutes, pushers and gang-bangers, who sometimes sought to use the premises for illicit/illegal purposes. Some might think it odd that I actually became friends with some of the clientele, once we agreed that they would "bring no heat" on the establishment; meaning, would not attempt to conduct any business while staying there.

If, "impressed", is the appropriate term, I would tell congregants in churches how impressed I was with the work ethic of dope dealers who, if they just channeled their talents in a legitimate direction, could probably succeed in, most, any field of endeavor. They never left a conversation, with anyone, without offering him, or her, a "dime bag", a "toot", a "hit" or a hustle (an opportunity to pick up a little sump'n, sump'n for "makin' a little run"). And, I do mean, never! Dealers would wave at cars going by, without fearing that they might be beckoning to law enforcers or stickup men, or women. They were "on the job", 24/7. I was the manager, working hard to keep stuff off the premises, and they would make offers to *me*, "just in case I wanted to 'check it out', maybe, this one time." After telling my story, my question to the Christians in these churches where the pastors were kind enough to allow me to speak, was, and continues to be, "What if we, as Christians, were equally as diligent in our attempts to be exemplary servants?"

The dope dealers **choose – yes, choose –** to be proficient at (attempting to) outsmart law enforcement and outwork us "squares" (1950s term for law abiding citizens) for illicit gain. You will hear the statement repeated, over and over again, by those who work to rehabilitate criminals – actual, and "wannabe" – "If they just **chose** to go straight, they could succeed at, most, anything."

I can see why Wanda would suggest that I use my story, here. American students of all backgrounds, and social orientations, acceptable or unacceptable to others, have the wherewithal to excel in whatever endeavors command their serious attention and hours – let us say, perhaps, ten thousand hours – of their concentrated time. Not only do I believe that this excellence can be achieved by choice, but I am hopeful that our American students will make that choice because they respect those who sacrifice for them, and because our students realize how much our nation needs their excellence in the classroom.

Students have parents, older siblings, other relatives, friends, mentors and folks they've never met, defending their right to get a free, quality, education in a safe and orderly environment. These heroes chose to put themselves in harm's way, from possible injury to possible death, because they believe that our nation is worth it. What student would dare tell a wounded warrior that he, or she, is not worth our best efforts in class?

The Video Series

"Thank you, NSCI, for challenging teachers to challenge learners."

In 1991, I was blessed to meet a gentleman whose name is Jerry George. As President of the National Schools Conference Institute (NSCI), headquartered in Phoenix, Arizona, Dr. George presided over several effective schools conferences each year. One of those conferences, the Annual Conference On Students "At-Risk," was, immediately, "my conference." It was certainly not, singularly, "my" (possessive) conference as, over years of being allowed to participate in this event, I met many educators, primarily administrators, who expressed a similar "ownership."

One administrator in particular, from Louisville, Kentucky, said to me, "I send teachers to various conferences, but, this one is 'my conference'." I – indeed, we – *claimed* the "At Risk" conference (later, titled, *Challenging Learners With Untapped Potential*) as our own because stellar presenters demonstrated, year after year, the high levels of accomplishment they were able to realize in, so-called, "lost" students. Presenters demonstrated myriad creative ways to prove that, indeed, "all students can learn"; yes, all students can exercise the choice to excel. Those of us who have spent our careers addressing this population were gratified, not only because so many presenters agreed that "all students can learn" (a phrase I'd like to attribute to whomever made it popular), but, also, because they gave us so very many ways – so many **choices** of ways – to motivate, and then teach, them how to achieve and sustain excellence. Teachers and students need only to, first, choose (make up their minds) to achieve at high levels, and then, secondly – and, eternally – follow a plan that satisfies this pursuit based upon the "personality" (i.e., theme, structure, leadership, demographics, size, resources, etc.) of their schools.

NSCI held annual conferences on Urban Education, Standards and Assessment, School to Career Tech Prep, Effective Schools, K-12 Integrated/Thematic Curriculum, and more, including the one addressing "Students At Risk". Every conference featured outstanding presenters. Every conference sent participants home, to their local districts, with notes, strategies, networks, materials and attitudes of confidence that enhanced their deliveries (by their own accounts) of best practices in very significant, even profound, professional ways. My appreciation for NSCI introducing me to "my conference" – one revealing several strategies to reach students "at-risk" – is borne out of the depth of knowledge I gained from colleagues in attendance, and the longevity of effectiveness of their approaches. I repeat: Surely, teachers, if they **choose** to adopt and apply what is available to them; and students, if they **choose** to get serious about their pursuit of excellence – cooperating with the teachers who have **chosen** to improve – both will become excellent immediately (as "performers"), and achieve excellence ultimately (as performers).

Among the educators who helped shaped the principles of high expectations being essential to students' academic achievement were those in attendance at a workshop I was allowed to conduct in the Dolton/Calumet, Illinois School District 149 in August, 1997. Led by Assistant Superintendent, John Martin Jones, the educational leaders, present, offered a more positive replacement for the term, "at-risk." They decided to use the term, "Learners With Untapped Potential." NSCI adopted the term in 1998. The conference title became, "Challenging Learners With Untapped Potential." (NSCI Vice President in 1999, Karen Young, with agreement from Dr. George, allowed me to become a part of the NSCI staff as Vice President of Urban Education).

Certainly, challenges, but also champions: An NSCI documentary series

Because of conference attendees' demand for more (more examples of excellence, more exposure to best practices in effective teaching, more opportunities to find replicable strategies for "tapping" under-performing students' potential), NSCI produced a video series featuring top educators in various offices and positions. The series, titled, Challenges and Champions, Urban Education In America[25], the brainchild of Dr. Walter Amprey, former Superintendent of Schools in Baltimore, MD, visited reformed schools from New York, New York, to Denver, Colorado and exposed viewers (target audience, classroom teachers and school administrators) to effective strategies for improving student achievement – from the classroom to school leadership to community involvement. You might use the information shared in the series in various ways:

• Consider the similarities of challenges, then and now;

• Determine what strategies are applicable, still, today;

• Search updated references to the featured practices and practitioners;

• Decide on strategies that better apply to your present situation.

• Choose to apply them as they were applied, where such application is relevant.

My references to the practices featured in the series are made to show some viewers, and to remind others, that educators have been finding creative ways to achieve excellence in difficult environments for a long time. These, turn-of-the-century, approaches were not new, conceptually, then, nor are they old, now. As students' personalities and teaching technology evolve, effective educators continue to find creative ways to "tap" students' potential. The fact that these examples of excellence focus on improving under-performing schools, or school districts, does not suggest that we should replicate only the dynamic strategies that are used in sensational "reform" cases.

Where schools have traditions of excellence that are sometimes overlooked because of their understated consistency, educators would be well-served to use models that fit the needs of their own situations. Media are often impressed by the "fantastic change" that occurs in an exciting case of reform. America must respect, and appreciate, the fact that excellent educators are not in the business of flaunting success for purposes of publicity. While we sensationalize the extreme, and point out where we are behind other nations, let us never forget the outstanding work being done, everyday, by dedicated American educators who are unsung, but undaunted. Yes, this book (about this campaign for academic patriotism) insists that we can, and must, do better; but, this insistence is put forward because so many of our practitioners are proving how great we are where myriad American educators, students and families have already made that choice.

Using examples from NSCI's "Challenges and Champions" video series, I invite you to consider why the proposition is put forth that excellence can be achieved by choice; and how and why we must, all, play a part in achieving that excellence. I offer these "proofs" of the possibilities of achieving academic proficiency in an order that shows a logical procession from believing to achieving. Twelve categories (The STOOTS, 12-Step Approach), flowing logically from one concept to the next, contain brief descriptions of strategies used in various school settings

Challenges and Champions:

Urban Education In American Schools

A Few Excerpts From the Series: Here, Using the Categories:

1. **Belief System**

2. **Leadership**

3. **Staff Development**

4. **Parental Involvement**

5. **Early Childhood Development**

6. **Literacy**

7. **Science and Technology**

8. **Assessment**

9. **Cultural Commonality**

10. **School wide / District wide**

11. **Community Involvement**

12. **Foundations and Grants**

When a school system secures agreement among its leaders that they have a shared **Belief System**, the **Leadership**, then, has the responsibility to conduct a **Staff Development** program that brings all professionals "on board." Now, together, leadership and staff must invite **Parental Involvement** that illustrates, both, an understanding and acceptance of the core beliefs. The progression from the school and home agreement on what drives their joint pursuit of academic achievement begins in the home, at the child's earliest stage of learning. At school, **Early Childhood Development** progresses through **Literacy** to advanced learning, including **Science and Technology** complementing core competencies, subjected to ongoing, regular, **Assessment.** America is a most inclusive society, and is often called upon to address cultural diversity. For this progression of categorical considerations from the video series, all that has been mentioned must include the vast population of families attending our schools. Rather than use the term, cultural diversity, I offer the term, **Cultural Commonality**. Excellence is expected from all American students, whoever they are, and from whatever backgrounds they come, and whether the practices are **School wide** or **District wide**. Successful schools invite **Community Involvement**. In most districts, resources abound, but too often, many are never solicited. Not only are there myriad in-kind contributions that can be tapped; but, there are multiple **Foundations** making financial **Grants** available in larger numbers than some of us can imagine. As we attempt to live up to our military's expectations of schools pursuing excellence with a sense of purpose complementary to their own, we offer a few excerpts of that ongoing pursuit on the video series we are describing, here. Permission has been granted to share the entire series with interested districts. Such presentations will reflect upon what was done when the series was filmed (1998) and bring you up to date. There are more examples than these from many excellent resources. You, no doubt, will create more of your own. I was allowed to be the host/moderator of the series.

(Use of video excerpts, with permission, for professional development presentations)

Chapter 9
When Adults Believe

1. Belief System

"...If you leave here with the word DUTY implanted in your mind; if you leave here with the word HONOR carved in your soul; if you leave here with love of COUNTRY stamped on your heart, then you will be a twenty-first century leader worthy... of the great privilege and honor...of leading...the sons and daughters of America... **General H. Norman Schwarzkopf**

The Efficacy Institute, Inc.

In the urban education video series, Dr. Jeffery Howard, Director of The Efficacy Institute, Inc. explains that "Efficacy is the capacity to mobilize the efforts of teachers, parents, and students, towards the achievement of successive, targeted learning outcomes."

His own view is, "The health of a community can be measured by its success in developing all of its children."

While this represents a belief system, it represents his personal belief system. And, this is good. Those responsible for sustaining the Efficacy Institute, Inc. adhere to the Efficacy Principle: *We must continually affirm for students the connection between their efforts and their achievements; they will get smart if they work hard.*

Their current (2014) web page speaks to their mission with these words: "For more than 25 years, the Efficacy Institute has been dedicated to the **mission** of getting all children to proficiency or higher. This is accomplished through a package for systemic education reform that involves a Mission, Mindset and Method."

Schools in Richmond, CA, Hattiesburg, MS and Memphis, TN are, but, a few featured on their website. They made the choice to accept the Efficacy belief system.

2. Leadership

"Great leaders are almost always great simplifiers, who can cut through argument, debate and doubt, to offer a solution everybody can understand." **General Colin Powell**

The Chancellor's District, New York Schools

In the introduction to this segment, my words were, "I'd like for you to imagine being responsible for the New York City School System: 1,116 schools; 1.1 million students; 66,000 teachers, and a budget of $8.8 billion." (1998).

Dr. Rudy Crew had that responsibility. As we consider leadership, the next words could be, "nuff said." But, the District identified 12 schools: six elementary, and six middle that needed intensive reform. A very good indicator that their improvement was dependent, largely, upon leadership was that they were "placed" (not geographically, but structurally) in The Chancellor's District. His leadership was critical to their reformation.

3. Staff Development

"Never lose touch with the troops. Remember that you serve the troops and it is the troops who matter. **Colonel R. Meinertzhagen**

The Paideia Institute of Hyde Park, Chicago, IL

"The idea is that students are empowered. They do not have to give the same answer as the teacher. They only have to substantiate their answer, based upon the only expert in the room, the text."

Dr. Robert D. Brazil, Director of Chicago's Paideia Institute of Hyde Park discussed one of the primary challenges, for teachers, of Socratic teaching. The students are empowered to offer opinions. Dr. Brazil's responsibility for helping as many as 40 schools, in the Chicago Public School District, rise above probation status prompted him to develop an institute that would give teachers the information and methodological strategies they needed to lift students' achievement levels. Considering his belief that students could learn better by engaging critical dialogue, he employed his skills as a leader to guide classroom teachers towards Socratic teaching from grade kindergarten to grade 12.

Sullivan High School Assistant Principal, Moses Vines said, "I found that I was learning as well as my students."

Grace Gedor, a junior at Sullivan, said, (the Socratic approach) "makes you a better thinker."

This was a great example of staff making a substantive change for significant improvement.

4. Parental Involvement

"By profession I am a soldier and take pride in that fact. But I am prouder – infinitely prouder – to be a father." **General Douglas MacArthur**

Park Hill Elementary International Studies Magnet School
Denver, CO

The importance of parental involvement is reflected in a statement that was made by Daniel S. Goldin, Administrator, National Aeronautics, Space Administration (N.A.S.A.): "We can't delegate the education of our children to someone else."

In this series segment it appeared that Goldin's words were "golden" to parents who challenged his challenge. Park Hill Elementary School became an International Studies Magnet School because parents decided to apply for a federal grant (which was, subsequently, "granted") that funded the reformation of this campus. Beth Briggs was the principal who believed enough in the parents, and their children, to lead the staff to follow the parents. It was one very good example of meaningful parental involvement.

Chapter 10
Students Achieve

5. Early Childhood Development

"I think that at a child's birth, if a mother could ask a fairy godmother to endow it with the most useful gift, that gift would be curiosity." **Eleanor Roosevelt**

Early Childhood Professional Development Network

"Early childhood experiences involve providing books…"

It is clear that there was more to the statement made by Carolyn Dorrell, Executive Director of the Early Childhood Professional Development Network, when she was interviewed for the video series. However, if parents and teachers simply followed Dr. Dorrell's (implied) directions, child development would, certainly, start early. The Early Childhood Professional Development Network continues to provide guidance for educators who engage children at their earliest stages of learning. Her words ("…providing books") can be used to segue, perfectly, into the next category.

6. Literacy

"The nation that makes a great distinction between its scholars and its warriors will have its thinking done by cowards and its fighting done by fools." **Thucydides**

Denver Public Schools, Denver, CO

Superintendent, Dr. Irv Moskowitz of Denver Public Schools explained components of their focus on literacy. He discussed frequent literacy testing, early grade reading assistance programs, tutoring, increased parental involvement and mandatory summer school (for students who did not meet the requirements to advance).

There are many (myriad) educational programs focusing on literacy. I can remember a requirement I had for teaching reading the first period of the day when I was a $7^{th}/8^{th}$ grade science teacher at Parkside Elementary School in Chicago, IL in 1973. All Chicago elementary school teachers were on alert as to the importance of literacy. Four decades later, the importance of addressing literacy at an early age is, even, more important than in 1973. Dr. Moskowitz addressed it in 1998. Denver's schools continue to implement strategies that address early, and sustained, literacy in all schools. (Among my experiences in teaching reading at the 8th grade level was an experience that involved having students read Shakespeare's Hamlet. We read it through, aloud, in class. After that first reading, I took the class to see the play as it was performed at Kennedy King Community College on Chicago's south side. You can imagine what our second reading yielded. Richard Burton, "eat your heart out!" Or, should that be, grammatically, "eat out your heart." Hmmm.)

7. Science & Technology

"I still need Marines who can shoot and salute. But I need Marines who can fix jet engines and man sophisticated radar sets as well." **General Robert E. Cushman, Jr.**

The National Research Council's

Center for Science, Mathematics & Engineering Education

At the time of our taping, Rodger Bybee was the Executive Director of the National Research Council's Center for Science, Mathematics & Engineering Education. While the Council's offices were in Washington, DC, Denver, Colorado's West High School commanded attention because their reform efforts focused on science and technology. Those who have participated in current, turn-of-the-century, STEM programs build their Science, Technology, Engineering and Math curricula on the late twentieth century projects and programs that enlightened the education, military, environmental, economic and other communities as to the importance, and practical applicability of technological phenomena and instruments. Iris Harp, a math teacher at West expressed appreciation for the "partnership" with the **National Science Foundation** as they encouraged more females and minority students to go into science and math.

8. Assessment

...Excellence in all we do.

One of US Air Force Core Values

L' Tanya Sloan, Ed. D

Dr. L' Tanya Sloan (Simmons) has expertise in many areas pertaining to improving schools, urban and beyond. As an Educational Consultant, Dr. Sloan assisted in the production of Challenges and Champions: Urban Education in America by explaining the importance of assessments being aligned with state standards. She spoke to the availability of software that covers grades kindergarten through 12, with applications suitable to all structures of individual schools, and school systems. The segment not only speaks to the importance, and availability, of tools to address constant and consistent feedback that is useful to teachers, students, and guardians, but it also shows the value in tapping the knowledge and tools of excellent consultants and other resources.

Chapter 11
And Communities Receive

9. Cultural Commonality

"There is not a liberal America and a conservative America – there is the United States of America. There is not a black America and a white America and Latino America and Asian America ... there's the United States of America."

President Barack Obama

Marine Park Middle School, Brooklyn, NY

As we focused on Cultural Diversity (again, I prefer to say, "Cultural Commonality"), we were allowed to use a film loaned to us by ("Courtesy of" -) Apple Staff Development, Apple Computer, Inc. Their documentary, within our documentary, introduced Ms. Mary Harrington (then) Acting Principal at Marine Park Middle School in Brooklyn, NY. She informed viewers of the fact that, at this one school, students spoke "50 different languages."

We heard Karen Penzell, 6th and 7th grade ESL teacher tell us that, "Ti from Cambodia, Raymond from China, Andrew from Russia, and Caroline from Venezuela are working together...

"English is the only lesson they all have in common.

"I tell my children they are twice as smart because they speak two languages."

Diversity/Commonality does not suggest that its relevance is authentic only when "50 languages" are spoken. We must seek to understand - and use creatively - differences in students' class, geography, passions, family structure, gifts, talents and much more. The more we know about our academic families (the children, and those with whom they live), the better we are able to serve them. And, by the way, the more they know about us, the more confident they'll be in "being themselves."

Thank you Apple Staff Development, Apple Computer, Inc.

10. Community Involvement

"You, you and you.... Panic. The rest of you, come with me."

US Marine Corps: Gunnery Sgt.

New American Schools, Arlington, VA

"It is also, we think, essential that the larger community – the business community, and other elements of that community – be engaged so that a change process can be sustained. Otherwise reform efforts, improvement efforts, come and go with political winds, with particular leadership..."

John Anderson, President of New American Schools, was commenting, both, on the city of Detroit, Michigan's Urban Systemic Initiative (see, below), and on community involvement as a concept. As a component of one particular program, USI, community involvement proved to be crucial. Placed in the context of stability, Dr. Anderson's remarks remind us that a single community can be subjected to several reforms - some effective, some, well, not so much. The changes come and go.

The community remains. There is always need for an astute community component for stabilization, even during change.

11. District Wide/School Wide

"An army is a team. It lives, eats, sleeps, fights as a team."

General George S. Patton

The Urban Systemic Initiative

Dr. Luther Williams of the National Science Foundation initiated a school reform effort, titled, The Urban Systemic Initiative (1993). Identifying the most impoverished school districts in America, USI promised $15 million, over a span of five years, for successful programs, with an emphasis on math and science.

The importance of looking at a program of this magnitude – there are USIs in cities across the nation – in 1998, and again, now, in 2014, is to point out that while individual schools (individual students) are admonished to make the choice to be excellent, that same choice can, and must, be made for education systems. Urban Systemic Initiative schools exist(-ed) in Baltimore, Chicago, Dallas, Detroit, Miami-Dade, New York, Phoenix, El Paso, TX and beyond. You may investigate their effectiveness by reviewing any number of analytical and evaluative reports, local and national. They are not the only schools that are included in district wide efforts. Economists, Greg J. Duncan of the School of Education at University of California at Irvine, and Richard J. Murnane of the Harvard Graduate School of Education complimented the Boston Public School pre-K program, the University of Chicago's K-12 Charter

119

School Network and New York City's small high schools of choice, as reported on by David Wessel in the Wall Street Journal in March, 2014.

The point to be made, here, is that, when a common belief system is embraced and followed by the other elements, above, effective approaches towards excellence in American schools can be implemented at all levels: School, cluster, sub-district, district, county, state and nation. Even when sub-districts are identified as needing greater reform concentration, because of their peculiar demographics or other factors, the entire district is always impacted by what they accomplish, or fail to accomplish. The smaller positive impact always lifts the larger system. We recall the words of President, John F. Kennedy, "A rising tide lifts all boats." I suggest that educated masses lift all classes. While the Urban Systemic Initiative was featured in the documentary, there are many programs to be scrutinized and considered for replication where you are. There is also opportunity for you to be creative in planning your own, new, school, or district, reform program

12. Foundations and Grants

"Ask not what your country can do for you - ask what you can do for your country."

President John F. Kennedy

Martin Luther King Efficacy Academy, Denver, CO

The Senior Producer for the video series, Challenges and Champions, was Glenn Meyers, a resident of Denver, CO. Because Mr. Meyers enjoys great respect in his community, we were fortunate to have the cooperation of the Denver Public Schools system for the taping of several episodes. Administrators and teachers at Martin Luther King Efficacy Academy were very candid about their need for intervention, and support, from a foundation based upon their needs.

Patricia Gatewood, Principal at King made the statement, "One of the problems any inner city school has to face is public image."

Math teacher Doug Tucker said, "About eight years back, a national TV (news magazine) program brought in hidden cameras to show everything that was wrong at Martin Luther King..."

It is interesting that an acute need to change the image at a local school (of course, among other significant concerns) spawned the establishment of a major foundation that helped the school improve much more than its image. Mr. Pat Hammill, a local business owner of Oakwood Homes, established the Foundation for Educational Excellence. The funds not only addressed the physical needs of the building, but they were also used for materials and equipment used inside of the building and for staff needed to lower teacher: pupil ratio. The funds purchased state of the art supplies and helped to create a national image for one local school that inspired similar programs, nationwide.

Sometimes, we fail to use available resources because we fail to search for them in our local communities. In this day of universal use of technology, a quick reference to topics on the Internet will help us find any number of foundations letting grants, often in the very category that addresses "our" needs. From time to time, it is a good idea – as local entrepreneur, Pat Hammill, proved in the case of Martin Luther King Efficacy

Academy – to knock on the door of your neighbor who happens to have a business.

CONCLUSION

The STOOTS for Boots Campaign asserts that excellence is available, in the forms of effective strategies and usable tools, all around us. We can choose to use them if we have the desire to do so. Most every educator is aware of that fact. What is not quite so comprehensible is that students, too, can choose excellence, and can attain and sustain same, if they desire to do so. The aim of the campaign is to provide students with the motivation to make the choice. It is our ardent belief that respect for the United States military is a legitimate motivating factor in causing under-performing students to choose to become excellent; and for achieving students to become, even, more determined to display American greatness. The examples of school reform cited here, from the video documentary produced by NSCI, show that change does come with the collective choice of school district personnel, working with students, parents and communities. The issue is to find, once the choice has been made, ways to enact similar reforms within the context of Academic Patriotism. Where adults believe, students achieve and the community receives assurance of a secure future.

Chapter 12
Instilling Academic Patriotism

The choice has been made. Not only have the school, district, organization, business and, most of all, family representatives, cited above, made the joint decision to make their schools excellent; but, in like, and updated, manner so have thousands of American stakeholders committed to improving the learning institutions serving their children. It is likely that every one of these learning institutions touts a belief system, most often expressed in the form of a mission statement. To introduce this chapter, I found the following three examples of school mission statements on the Internet:

Mountain Gap Middle School

Huntsville, AL

THE MISSION OF MOUNTAIN GAP MIDDLE SCHOOL IS TO PROVIDE EACH STUDENT A DIVERSE EDUCATION IN A SAFE, SUPPORTIVE ENVIRONMENT THAT PROMOTES SELF-DISCIPLINE, MOTIVATION AND EXCELLENCE IN LEARNING. THE MOUNTAIN GAP TEAM JOINS THE PARENTS AND COMMUNITY TO ASSIST THE STUDENTS IN DEVELOPING SKILLS TO BECOME INDEPENDENT AND SELF-SUFFICIENT ADULTS WHO WILL SUCCEED AND CONTRIBUTE RESPONSIBLY IN A GLOBAL COMMUNITY.[26]

Centennial High School

Ellicott City, MD

IT IS CENTENNIAL HIGH SCHOOL'S MISSION TO PROVIDE A SAFE, NURTURING ENVIRONMENT THAT DEVELOPS RESPONSIBILITY, PERSONAL INTEGRITY, SELF-RESPECT, AND RESPECT FOR OTHERS; THAT NURTURES A DESIRE TO BECOME A LIFELONG LEARNER, THAT FOSTERS A SENSE OF COMMUNITY; WHILE APPRECIATING OUR DIVERSE CULTURAL HERITAGE; AND THAT UPHOLDS AN EMPHASIS ON ACADEMIC AND PERSONAL EXCELLENCE. [27]

Avenues – The World School
New York, NY

WE WILL GRADUATE STUDENTS WHO ARE ACCOMPLISHED IN THE ACADEMIC SKILLS ONE WOULD EXPECT; AT EASE BEYOND THEIR BORDERS; TRULY FLUENT IN A SECOND LANGUAGE; GOOD WRITERS AND SPEAKERS ONE AND ALL; CONFIDENT BECAUSE THEY EXCEL IN A PARTICULAR PASSION; ARTISTS NO MATTER THEIR FIELD; PRACTICAL IN THE WAYS OF THE WORLD; EMOTIONALLY UNAFRAID AND PHYSICALLY FIT; HUMBLE ABOUT THEIR GIFTS AND GENEROUS OF SPIRIT; TRUSTWORTHY; AWARE THAT THEIR BEHAVIOR MAKES A DIFFERENCE IN OUR ECOSYSTEM; GREAT LEADERS WHEN THEY CAN BE, GOOD FOLLOWERS WHEN THEY SHOULD BE; ON THEIR WAY TO WELL-CHOSEN HIGHER EDUCATION; AND, MOST IMPORTANT, ARCHITECTS OF LIVES THAT TRANSCEND THE ORDINARY. [28]

There are similarities in the three statements, above, regarding such important matters as academic efficiency, diversity, safety and community. As it regards academic efficiency, Mountain Gap includes the words, ... *excellence in learning*; Centennial, ...*an emphasis on academic and personal excellence*; and Avenues: ... *accomplished in the academic skills.*

On diversity: Mountain Gap - ... *a diverse education*; Centennial - ... *our diverse cultural heritage*; Avenues - ... *truly fluent in a second language.*

Safety: Mountain Gap - ....*in a safe, supportive environment;* Centennial - ...*pro-vide a safe, nurturing environment*; Avenues - ...*emotionally unafraid and physically fit.*

And, Community: Mountain Gap - ...*the parents and community*; Centennial - ... *a sense of community*; and, Avenues - ... *aware that their behavior makes a difference in our ecosystem.*

While each school has unique qualities, personnel and populations, all schools have – or, should have – some very important common principles such as those illustrated above. Because of shifts in leadership, global concerns, community needs, current enlightenment or, sometimes, popular trends, education systems may change their mission statements to be relevant in a given era, but certain concepts, as discussed above, remain common among most education systems.

I would hope that in the near - and permanent - future, every American school's mission statement will include a passage that honors our United States of America military.

On Academic Patriotism

A New Look At an Old Book. Thank You, Waco, Texas

In my, 2006 (copyright, 2004, released 2006), book, *The 5th Front Campaign – How Every American Can Engage Our Global Struggle By Supporting Our Schools,*[29] I introduced the STOOTS concept. Three of the five ways that I related academic "stoots on the ground" to military boots on the ground (pages 165-166) were: 1. "Stoots on the ground" will make the connection of academic excellence to patriotism, 3. "Stoots on the ground" will provide our military with a real-time, tangible, attestation to the reason for their sacrifices: to protect the students who must secure our future, and 5. "Stoots on the ground" will show the world that, when American youths make up their minds to excel, no one, no thing, no foe, no campaign, no threat of terror – present or potential – can stifle their success.

I changed the term, "Stoots on the ground", to the acronym, STOOTS, which stands for Students' Theater Of Operations, The School. As suggested in my, "*5th Front*", title, I sought to launch a campaign involving all American civilians who desired to actively, and meaningfully, support our troops. I felt – and, I still feel – that there is no more important way to show respect for the sacrifices service personnel make than to secure their futures, with academic excellence, as they secure our freedoms, with duty and honor. Our children are their future. Our children in school are their secure future, provided that they excel in school. Indeed, our children are America's future.

In my travels to schools across America, I was honored to visit Waco, Texas, in 2007. My visit was hosted by the Cen-Tex African American Chamber of Commerce, whose President was

Ms. Laveda Brown. Because of my purpose for writing *The 5th Front Campaign,* the city of Waco was gracious enough to allow me to "kick off" my campaign, there, in October of that year. Seven years later, I feel that I owe Waco, Texas an encouraging update. The school district that is mentioned in the acknowledgements section of that book, the Hickman Mills School District, Kansas City, Missouri, was "the first to allow me to present this concept". On May 15, 2014 a press conference was held at the Hickman Mills District's Ruskin Senior High. Our "STOOTS for Boots" Campaign – which is an outgrowth from The 5th Front Campaign – asked students to dedicate this 2014-2015 school year to American servicemen and women. Each of the first 28 students to volunteer said, verbatim, or some variation of, "Because of your sacrifice to defend our nation, I am serious about my education."

This chapter dealing with instilling academic patriotism seeks to keep you from having to spend seven years developing an outline, and securing human and material resources, to invite, engage – even, excite – student commitment to excellence in honor of our troops. In fact, our invitation to students seeks to engage and excite them about seeking to be excellent as Americans. We request students' commitment to excellence on behalf of – not, to – American servicewomen and men. The commitment is to the nation. The catalyst is a profound respect, and admiration, for the courage and attention to duty of our troops. Asking students to be serious, "for your country", is sometimes seen as "corny", "old fashioned", "square", by young people, particularly adolescents and teens, who are fearful of negative peer pressure. Those very same young people are empowered when seen in proximity to uniformed heroes during their surprise visits to schools.

Instilling Academic Patriotism: The Invitation

Of the millions of American teachers serving our nation in schools across the country, very few have neglected to extend this invitation, in one form, or another, regularly. We arrive, for the most part, for the, very, most part, in front of classrooms out of a desire to make our country better by making better the lives of our charges, and their families. The social and political climate of today's society seems to discourage, or "play down", overt expressions of patriotism by educators in our classrooms. Often, out of fears similar to those felt by adolescents concerning peer pressure, plus concerns about lawsuits, classroom teachers opt to be more "politically correct" than patriotically erect. But, let us not be disillusioned. Teaching in America is a patriotic profession. The invitation to students to be excellent for our nation is extended to millions of students, by millions of American teachers, everyday! Unequivocally! Unashamedly!

For some reason, young people seem to be more willing to do things for friends, mentors and coaches than for themselves. I have worked with young people who claimed gang affiliation. Some claimed to be murderers. As educators – particularly, those of you who work with pre-teens and teens – we know that many of the bravado claims are from "wannabe's". (However, let us be careful to take every boast seriously, reporting the pronouncements to proper authorities, out of caution for "that one time" when the threat proves to be real). During the early 1980s and into the '90s, there was a rash of "drive-by" shootings, especially in urban communities. I was asked to "work with" some young people in Kansas City, Missouri, as that was one of the locations experiencing youth violence. I remember conducting a teachers' staff development session in which a colleague asked a question, supported by responses of agreement from others. The question was, "Mr. Boyd, don't you think they'd stop the killing if we could convince them that they're only killing themselves?"

My response was: "Actually, I don't think so. Part of their street credibility is looking such appeals in the eye, and claiming "no fear". These young folks have ready answers for, 'Don't you know you're killing yourselves?'

"They will say (whether owning it, or not) such things as: 'Everybody's got to die.' 'You could die crossing the street.' 'I don't intend to live that long, anyway.' 'I can't go 'round being afraid to get killed. Hey, that's to be expected.' 'You can't be a (name of gang), and not expect to die', etc.

"I find greater success when I appeal to them by saying (something like), 'I know you've got your lifestyle, and, though I love you like my own son, I might not be able to change you. I just need your help with (his/her friend). You know how much potential he, or she, has, and we need you to help us save him, or her."

It's "funny" how the individual's attitude adjusts to this new appeal. Often – really, often – young miscreants have not only given strategies to "get to" (friend), but they often participate in helping. Of course, you and I know that the desired outcome is for this individual to change, as well, "on his/her own." And, it does happen, many times.

Now, we know that every American student should be patriotic because of the freedoms they enjoy, including the rights and privileges of an American (the greatest) education. But, when they don't seem to grasp the importance of having this opportunity, perhaps we can encourage them to be patriotic for "friends" who sacrifice for their rights.

Instilling Academic Patriotism: The Engagement

Ceremonies can be stirring. Witness the orchestral arrangements, and fireworks, accompanying celebrations on the White House lawn during military holidays.

Surprise visits can be touching. Even the most cynical individual must admit to being moved when mom, or dad, appears in the audience, or comes from behind the curtain, or removes the school mascot attire, appearing in uniform, to embrace sons and daughters after returning home from a war zone.

"Welcome Home" greetings can be celebratory when entire schools turn out at a local airport to greet units of local service personnel arriving at 2:00 a.m.

VA hospital visits are heartfelt. Consider the first steps, after rehab, taken by a former coach who was wounded in battle, being witnessed by the high school team he had led to a championship.

Students invited to express their patriotism with excellence are, often, encouraged by such events as these, and many other similar events, for at least as long as the occasion lasts. After they have participated in a stirring, touching and/or heartfelt, celebration, we are not surprised when students are heard to say, "I'm going to make them proud," or some other, such, statement. The fact that the promise is not always kept does not mean the intent was not there when it was made. Commitments need to be reinforced, regularly. They need to be made within the context of an action that lasts longer than a single occasion. And, the likelihood of a commitment being kept is strengthened by the engagement, in that action, of more than one person.

The STOOTS For Boots Campaign thanks and congratulates all of the educators who have motivated students towards academic patriotism since well before I began my career, in 1964, and those who will be on the front lines of that motivation well after I have finished my course. The strength and power of this campaign will not be realized in its originality. American educators are way out front, conceptually. The strength of the campaign comes with placing concept in a current context. Occasions will be observed within the context of a broader statement.

In a six-day span, from June 30th thru July 4th, 2014, three major occasions were celebrated (among many others). On June 30th a new center for homeless veterans opened in Kansas City, Missouri with appropriate ceremony. On July 2nd, Admiral Michelle Howard was announced to have become the highest ranked female in U.S. Navy history. On the Fourth of July, President, and First Lady, Obama welcomed military heroes and their families to the White House.

I did not see, at any of these ceremonies, coverage of conspicuous participation on the part of American students. From now on, because of their ongoing commitment to heroes such as these, it will be good to see American students present, expressing the sentiment – perhaps displaying placards with the caption – "Another Reason We Must Excel!" The engagement of students in activities that focus on the United States Armed Forces should not be designed to draw attention away from our military and, more, towards the students. The presence, and support, of the students should become common enough that media will, simply, remind viewers of the constant presence of American students, once again showing support, "here and, as always, in the classroom." It should also become common for service personnel to expect "STOOTStudents" to be present.

Instilling Academic Patriotism: The Excitement

American students participating in the "STOOTS for Boots" Campaign may enjoy a new relationship with American military personnel in formal and/or informal ways. Inasmuch as the campaign is not a recruitment campaign, designed to enlist students into a branch of the United States Armed Services, supportive activities need not be military-oriented. It is important – it is crucial – that all American students (so many of whom are already "All American" students) understand that their academic excellence in core subjects, in class, strengthens the global presence of our military, everywhere. Our forces need to (they have to) know that, wherever they confront enemies, the world's strongest nation in academics – which we must become – has their backs.

Therefore, whether as members of a formal JROTC, or of a STOOTS For Boots-type High School Club, when making such a statement as, "Because of your sacrifice to defend our nation, I am serious about my education," American students can back up such statements in one, or more, exciting ways. Once they become engaged in the concept of academic patriotism, you, as their teachers, might guide them to consider, but not limit themselves to, participating in such activities as:

1. STOOTS for Boots Clubs;

2. "Thank You" student rallies and assemblies for local military heroes;

3. Appearing at military events and ceremonies, when open to the public, with signs;

4. Visiting veterans' hospitals with assurances: "You were not wounded in vain;"

5. "Welcome Home" airport rallies, waving excellent grade cards;

6. Appearing on TV Public Service Announcements (PSAs) reciting commitment;

7. Calling Press Conferences to announce school academic patriotism activities;

8. STOOTS "Dream STEAM" Challenge

9. School-Veteran Partnership Program

10. Joint Appearances at athletic events: "We support our heroes" on jumbo-trons;

11. Students as guests at historic military bases "feel trips"

12. Rap Sessions with military personnel on our academic standing in the world;

13. "Back to School" Parades with school and military units ("A National...");

14. "STOOTS For Boots Camp" before school reconvenes;

15. Supportive social media interaction (properly, and carefully, monitored);

16. Appearing as guests on STOOTS TV, and/or other TV, programs;

17. Community Service Food and Clothing Drives for Veterans, with school theme;

18. Joint Color Guard presentations at school convocations;

19. Boots and Books Veterans as Mentors Programs;

20. "Your Nation Needs You" (YNNY) Veterans Against Violence;

21. "Stars and Skypes" Together: motivational military exchange with students;

22. Local Productions of "The Keeping Pace, at Home, Space" Challenge TV Show;

23. Academic Patriotism Day;

24. A's for Wounded Warrior Month

25. Student Stars Academic Patriotism Pledge Flag

If none of these is exciting enough, but, you'd still like to express your academic patriotism, please do so. An explanation of each of our recommended 25 activities, listed above, follows in Chapter 13.

Chapter 13
Activating Academic Patriotism

1. The "STOOTS for Boots" Club

The Statement: "Because of your sacrifice to defend our nation, I am serious about my education."

The Slogan: "Your Boots, Our Books!"

The Song: "We Must Learn as Heroes Fight!"

Should a school form a STOOTS For Boots Club, the Statement, Slogan and Song used to open each meeting are designed to set a tone of seriousness about "the business at hand." That "business", of course, is helping each other excel, academically, in honor of America's military. STOOTS T-shirts, caps, lapel pins and binders may be worn, and used, but are not requirements for membership. We require no dues, but look for these "do's" from a minimum of 28 members:

Allow names to be counted in the "STOOTS for Boots" Campaign;

Conduct at least one activity, per school year, in honor of American service personnel;

Send members' academic progress reports to STOOTS website;

Study as a group, together, at least once per week;

Support with your attendance at, least, one public military event (e.g., a Veterans Day Concert) per year.

The STOOTS for Boots Club may sponsor some of the activities listed below; or members may participate in other events as a club.

Please keep in mind that the STOOTS For Boots Campaign does not recruit for the armed services. We are a civilian effort to show proper respect for those who sacrifice for us.

2. "Thank You" Rallies

It is an honor to have military personnel attend school events, especially when they show up in their uniforms. It is a good thing when schools keep veterans and active duty members on their guest lists for every public event. Educators are happy to share the mutual joy comes from this permanent relationship. Armed Forces members will tell you that invitations to activities, from schools to servicewomen and men, are, in themselves, appreciated expressions of "Thank you for your service."

Once in a while, it is good, and proper, to create an occasion that is specifically *for* our military heroes. The "Thank You", in fact, may name the event. The title, the special guests, the presentations, the music, the entire program is designed to assure all of these honorees that their sacrifices are not made in vain. Proclamations may be read, certificates may be awarded and student speeches may be made. Surprise gifts may be given, and slide shows may be presented. Whatever the presentation; at this, particular, program, the school is taking "this moment" to do one thing for servicemen and women. At least once a year, we must say, "Thanks."

3. "Another Reason We Must Excel!"

The caption, above, may be placed on placards that appear in the crowd at a military parade, or in the seats at a military ceremony. Of course, the caption may be the STOOTS statement: "Because of your sacrifice to defend our nation, I am serious about my education." ("... *we* are serious about *our*...").

The creativity of American students presents endless possibilities for public expressions of admiration and respect for America's military. The suggestion, here, is to continuously seek ways to relate academic effort to military sacrifice. At every opportunity, we must remind our troops that we are ever vigilant in seeking to lead the world academically as we are aware of who makes it possible for us to cultivate that leadership. We hear interviews and read biographies from successful figures making it known that, "every chance I get", that they will never forget the sacrifices their parents made. In some cases, it was a surrogate parent, or teacher, or coach, or counselor, or very dear friend who made their success possible. But, whoever it was, they remind those figures, and all who will listen to stories about them, that they will never be forgotten. Students must also remember that the sacrifices of servicemen and women are ongoing. Perhaps a caption should, simply, read, "We'll never forget!"

As slogans are created, and signs are made, students can enjoy the process as well as the outcome. Putting thought into the display should result in a respectful work of which, both, the designer and the persons being honored, can feel proud. The class to be displayed by those in class will dictate when, where and how often these renderings should be visible. The idea is to show who is communicating the message more than what the message communicates. Let America know, continually, that students are striving for excellence to do their parts in our global struggle for leadership that is just, and leadership that is proficient. Every sacrifice made by America's military is another reason students must excel.

4. "You were not wounded in vain."

Perhaps a whisper in a wounded warrior's ear by a sincere high school student will be enough to motivate one more step on a walker. Perhaps a speech chorus of adolescents addressing a room full of amputees will help them – at least for that moment – forget the wound and remember the reason. However it is communicated during students' visits to hospitals treating our wounded servicemen and women, let the message come across, loud and clear, that American students are not "playing around" in school while their courageous parents, brothers and sisters, friends, mentors, coaches, even warriors who do not know them, are risking their very lives to keep the students safe enough to attend school.

Not all visits have to be lengthy. Not all statements have to be profound. Hospitalized warriors just need to know that outside of these walls are young people within academic walls taking seriously what "caused me to be here." There is no greater assurance of that fact than to have students, themselves, make occasional visits of reassurance to Veterans' Administration hospitals.

If students – and their teachers, and their parents – ever need a motivational boost, just let a hospitalized veteran tell them, in person, "I thank you for your excellence."

5. "Welcome Home"

To see groups of students at airports welcoming home returning troops is not unusual. It is not unusual to see them waving flags and/or waving creative signs on placards. STOOTS

For Boots would like to witness students waving grade cards with excellent grades and creative signs expressing promises of extra effort in honor of valiant warriors. The "war cry", if you will, "Your Boots, Our Books", should let service members know, not only how serious American students are about school, but should also help to make the association between serious confrontation in combat and serious calculation in class.

Every returning hero needs to see in the welcome gathering some evidence of commitment, on the part of students, to the betterment of the community they left behind. Even when the terrain is pristine, the work is plentiful and community residents are healthy, a student can say, "For you", I improved my attendance. Another can display a certificate received "because I was inspired by your unit's example of efficiency." A school athletic team might show a poster-sized photo of the players holding their 1st Place award in front of a large banner displaying the returning unit's patch.

While STOOTS clubs open meetings with the Statement ("Because of your sacrifice to defend our nation, **we** are serious about **our** education."), the Slogan ("Your Boots, Our Books"), and the Song ("We Must Learn As Heroes Fight"), they don't have to be members for students (parents, teachers and others) to repeat, enthusiastically, over and over, wherever troops are present "Your Boots, Our Books!"

Please do not stop celebrating troops' homecomings in ways you have done for decades. Many "Welcome Home" ceremonies have become traditions, and there is no need to change them. We only ask that you add context to tradition that allows for associating commitment to academics with commitment to military duty. And, of course, where no particular tradition exists, we strongly advocate creating one (or two, or three) that convinces every returning member of American Armed Forces that, while they're on battle fronts, American schools have their backs. There should come a time when ceremonies celebrating military personnel that do not include academic patriotism will seem incomplete; indeed, will *be* incomplete.

6. PSAs

PSAs are Public Service Announcements. Perhaps, for our nation's students, they should also be, Promises to Strengthen America! Visualize, if you will, a television split screen, showing on one side a warrior lifting a comrade while saying, "We'll never leave without you." On the other side of the split screen visualize a student trying hard to figure out a problem (or conduct an experiment, or access an app..), surrounded by classmates who are there to help, saying, "We'll never achieve without you." Now, with the warrior on one side of the screen and the students on the other, facing the camera, we see, and hear, the students say, "Because of your sacrifice to defend our nation, we are serious about our education." The statement remains the same. The variations of actions and captions are endless. TV has reach. Let the repetition teach.

7. The Press Conference

Calling press conferences should require that the subject be one of substance. News coverage does not always cover news; or, so it seems. Many segments that are featured on TV "news stations" appear to be more appropriate for talk shows or "funniest videos." Before requesting coverage of a "Press Conference", please consider the newsworthiness of the event. Though originality does not have to be a criterion for determining newsworthiness (after all, a fire is a fire, but all of them are most always newsworthy), we should respect our outlets enough to give them material that is worth showing. There are times when certain events/activities/announcements are not covered because they are pre-empted by something that is "more important."

Stories about servicemen and women showing up at their children's schools – by surprise – have been done, over and over again. They are said to be actualities that "never get old". But, you can let it be known that there is more to service–student relations than surprise visits (and, no, they don't get old, so please keep doing them). But, The Community Toolbox[30], a community service "how to" on the Internet, tells us that "A press conference is a tool designed to generate news – in particular, hard news ("a story in the print or electronic media which is timely, significant, prominent and relevant."). It goes on to say that you and your organization should hold a press conference:

When the event includes a prominent individual

When you have a significant announcement to make

When a number of groups are participating in an action...[31]

When Admiral Howard comes to your school to congratulate students for their achievement, a press conference would be in order. When the local National Guard is going to join you in conducting a STOOTS for Boots Camp, you should announce it at a press conference. When we kickoff the National Back to School Parade Day, a press conference is in order.

You will (hopefully) have several events and activities involving academic patriotism that are timely, significant, prominent and relevant. They are, and will be, worthy of coverage on their own merit. The additional reason for calling attention to these occasions is to keep the idea of students "doing their part" out of respect for America's military on the minds of the public as much as the pupils. We must all help educators to remind American students, regularly, that they, too, are heroes for honoring America by achieving in class as our troops represent us with class.

8. STOOTS " Dream STEAM " Challenge

Two students working with two servicemen and/or women comprise a four-member "STOOTS Dream STEAM" This annual event will feature student-military partnerships competing in aspects of Science, Technology, Engineering, Arts and Math as teams.

9. Veteran-Student Partnerships

However they might manifest, let the ongoing relationship between veterans and students mark an active appreciation for their complementary roles. Academic patriotism is a statement about student (indeed, school) respect for the sacrifices of warriors being shown by the students taking school seriously. More than the statement, there must be action among students that yields substantive proof of respect. To paraphrase a Biblical verse, "Statements without works are dead."[32]

Some veteran-student relations will manifest in formal mentor programs in which, after appropriate screening, will allow veterans to have regular (i.e., weekly or monthly) sessions with students they are helping to improve such things as their grades, attitudes, attendance and/or talents. Another interaction might include publishing a joint newsletter that keeps students motivated to have good reports, and keeps veterans motivated to understand today's youth. Students and veterans may have a single encounter per school year, at an outside major event, at a pre-graduation congratulations from the military to the students, at an annual outing, on a student "feel trip" or any of a number of interactions. Where there are annual STOOTS/Boots Back-to-School parades, there will be students (STOOTS) and veterans (Boots), as well as available active duty personnel.

Our repetitive call for academic patriotism is designed to force America to encourage our students to keep in mind their important global role as exemplary scholars. This repetition, these ongoing relations, should lead to this relationship becoming the norm, the expected, the tradition of all American schools. American veterans must know – we must continually let them know – how important they are in creating the climate for excellence in American schools. They made them possible. We must thank them with exemplary world leadership in our schools. An ongoing opportunity for students to show their gratitude to veterans will be found in developing and keeping a relationship between "STOOTS" and "Boots."

10. "We Support Our Heroes!"

All military-appreciation activities need not be lengthy or intricate. Please contact your local professional sports franchises. Arrange a "day" to celebrate the school-military relationship. This is different from celebrating the military, alone. Such celebrations are appropriate and, for certain, well deserved. They, too, should enjoy high attendance among students and their families (Memorial Day, Veterans' Day, Flag Day, Armed Forces Day, etc.). But, on particular days, determined by the local school, or school district, please ask permission to celebrate "STOOTS For Boots Day" (perhaps using another title, but expressing the same sentiment such as, "Academic Patriotism Day"); a day that celebrates associating   excellence in school with respect for warriors. Ask them to determine, a particular time (inning, time out, pre-game …) to show, on the large screen,(the "jumbo-tron") panning the stands, students' large posters, placards and banners that express admiration for the service, and commitment of warriors from students. Brief, creative, phrases with artistic illustrations would be great. The screen should show the students with military units.

11. Historic Military "Feel Trips"

I wrote the book, *Plain Teaching*,[33] in 1991. The subtitle is *49 Lessons On Becoming A Positive Teacher.* Based upon my – then - 27 years in the field of education, I discussed the expertise of colleagues who were outstanding teachers, and related some of my own experiences. Listed as Lesson Number 37[34] was the title, Plan And Take "Feel Trips." I suggested that "feel trips" are more participatory than field trips. This is not unusual to teachers in today's age of high tech equipment and phenomena, for, in 2014, a trip to a museum or space station would not be worth the preparation and travel without it being "hands on."

In discussing STOOTS for Boots "Feel Trips" with Sanah Bittaye, a young lady I've known since she was in high school, I found myself being reminded of "what Mom does." Sanah's mom, Lillian Bittaye, has been working with students, as a mentor, tutor, fund-raiser and toy distributor (for underserved communities) for decades. Miss Bittaye suggested that Mrs. Bittaye coordinate historic military "feel trips."

Even as I thought we should seek to engage students in the "more participatory" trips which would strengthen such relationships as mentioned in 9, above – Veteran-Student

Partnerships; but, to include active duty "partners", as well – Ms. Bittaye had been talking to Mom about the fact that many students are not motivated to learn about phenomena with which they have no historical connection. Their conversation had nothing to do with me. This was something they felt was needed, and were contemplating how to create the connection. An Atlanta citizen, Sanah contacted my wife, and me, on a visit to Kansas City. Catching up, I told her about my STOOTS For Boots campaign. She told me what her family had been discussing. The rest is – I hope – (military) history.

In the spirit of the "feel trip", we ask that you allow Lillian Bittaye to arrange for an historic excursion to an historic base, a vessel, a memorial ground or other military landmark where personnel will not only explain the history of the visit's focus, but will also make the connection with what young people are – or should be – doing today. If you have been doing this, already, or plan to do it outside of our campaign, we'd appreciate your allowing us to report what you have done, are doing and/or plan to do on our stootsforboots.com website.

12. Dialogue: "Your Nation Needs You"

Parents are not the only adults who become frustrated when their children (seem to) listen to others more attentively than to them. Teachers experience the same attitudes among "their" students. You will hear us say things such as, "Coach, you need to talk to your girl, here." "Charles, you better 'tighten up' your partner before he gets expelled." "Maybe they need a 'Scared Straight' encounter." "Who is a positive celebrity we can get to talk to them?"

Neither parents, nor teachers, need be ashamed. We are not failures. We are victims of the simple psychological phenomenon in adolescents – in fact, in human beings of all ages – that sees the need for acceptance and approval from perceived popular or strong figures, in our lives, who exist beyond the demands, or even requests, of those who "are 'always' trying to make us do something". I need help as I try to understand it, but it seems, sometimes that young people do not just hear their parents and teachers, they even agree with them. They just don't want you to know it. How often have you observed a child's enthusiastic response to a visitor, reacting as though it's the first time they've heard something, and heard yourself remarking, "I've said that very same thing a million times."

Well, there are heroes, and there are true heroes. Watch what happens when students engage a conversation with someone in the military, especially when that person is in uniform. Even if they are not in uniform, but an appropriately detailed introduction paints a picture of their heroism, students, and faculty, will pay rapt attention. Please allow dialogue between students and troops. Conduct at least one session per school year on the heroes' perspectives of the importance of American leadership. No American warrior should ever face danger with a feeling that an enemy thinks lowly of him, or her - not because of military weakness, but because that enemy believes America will crumble "from the school-side, out."

Considering our highlights on Socratic teaching, from the TV documentary series discussed in Chapter 8, let these sessions reflect the best style of the Socratic seminar. Let students engage their guests. Let them ask hard questions and put forth compelling arguments from wherever their inquiring minds come. But, let them come away from the dialogue with a clear understanding that, when American students compare poorly with foreign competitors, they let down those who fight for us. Even if they are not uttering the exact words, or using the phrase as a title, the military guests are saying, by implication, "Your nation needs you" to American students. Let these sessions be the school-site version of the "feel trip." From students to staff to administration to parents, everyone present who is not military should come away with a deep understanding of our patriotic obligation to excel.

13. THE Back To School Parade

Many school districts conduct "Back To School" parades. It is when local military units participate that, not only do these units add the appearance of "spit and polish" to the celebration, but they also add the best marching bands in the land. Please have viewers in the crowd display signs of gratitude and messages of the relationship between STOOTS and Boots. In the gatherings before the parade begins, and after the parade concludes, engage conversations that assure our warriors of the motivation they spark that helps students strive for excellence.

Among the "fun" aspects of the parade might be a float contest. A panel comprised of district administrators and parents/ guardians can give awards for "most appropriate symbols" (of service-school partnership), "best design", "most interactive" or whatever the panel decides. The prizes might include awards for marching units and signs and banners that appear along the parade route. As considerations to make the parade exciting are discussed, please let the excitement be as much about the relationship as about the activities.

"STOOTS for Boots" would love to see the back to school parade become **THE** back to school parade. From Washington, DC to Washington State, from Idaho Falls, Idaho to Oklahoma City, Oklahoma, on a particular day in August or September there should be **THE National Back to School Parade!** Through social media, stootsforboots.com would be happy – overjoyed – to share this event with the world. What a statement we would make when school districts, large and small, boasting American Cultural Commonality are displayed for everyone to see celebrating American academic unity.

Remember, the parade is a "Kickoff" event. It is not an end unto itself. Make it exciting. Make it inclusive. Make it national. Yes, make it fun. But, make it function to make a statement about intentions. "We are excited about how high we are going to rise during 'this' school year. If you think we're excited, now; wait until you see the celebration, at the end of the year, when we top the world in achievement!"

14. The "STOOTS For Boots Camp"

In section, #12, above, that dealt with Dialogue, we discussed students being impressed with uniformed heroes. One reason for their being impressed might be related to the mystique behind the uniform. Students may wonder if movies and TV specials "do justice" to the realities confronted by troops, from basic training to dangerous deployment. One way to give students an experience "beyond the parade" would be to ask military personnel to invite the students to a "STOOTS For Boots Camp."

This jointly planned (school, military and STOOTS) experience would include exercises requiring academic, as well as physical, discipline; and activities that help students learn the meanings of "rigor and relevance." For two-to-five days, depending upon the desires of the district, participants will be shown the direct relationship between developing, and practicing, great classroom habits and the way troops have had to develop, and practice, great combat habits. The camp might culminate on parade day.

15. Social Media, Serious Messages

As today's American students are inundated with social media games, gadgets and gimmicks, the cliché that ends with the words, "...join them" ("If you can't fight 'em, join 'em.") speaks loudly to all who desire to command the attention of young people (including young adults). We "can't fight them," nor should we want to. Some clear advantages of using social media are found in their immediacy, their reach, their presentation; and, yes, in their continuing "freshness."

STOOTS For Boots will make every effort to assure that all interactions are appropriate for the central theme (again, academic patriotism) and for the age range of those who "come online." It is important that the culture of patriotic parallelism, reflecting how we feel about our nation, and how we feel about our schools securing its future, be protected from trivial exchanges or, worse, disrespectful or inappropriate entries. An inspirational message or motivational passage, communicated on a given day, at a given time, may just come at a moment that ignites a lifetime of excellence.

Not only do we ask that interaction be allowed, but we encourage lively updates when reports are being made about such things as:

A "troop-tutored" A+ on an anticipated difficult exam;

A challenging day at a STOOTS Boot Camp;

A change in attitude from "the school bully" because of a troop mentor;

Plans of a trip to a vessel or a base;

Results of a STOOTS "Dream STEAM" challenge;

Defining of roles for an upcoming school-service activity;

A note of "congratulations" for a STOOTS/Boots accomplishment;

The military dignitary(-ies) who "showed up" at school, today;

Team collaboration in preparation for a lab presentation; or,

Announcement of a "flash JOB" to help repair a storm victim's home.

Of course, you, and your students – perhaps, especially, your students – will be far more creative than I; but, there is an imperative that interactions, representing this concept be appropriately representative.

16. STOOTS TV

While the "STOOTS for Boots" Campaign desires to air our own TV program, STOOTS students do not need to wait until we are in production to appear as guests on local programs (or, for that matter, national programs) discussing academic patriotism. In fact, students who profess no affiliation with this campaign, if they are conceptually tied to the concept, should be given opportunities to show our nation that our future rests in the best of hands. We would love, also, to see troop members on TV discussing how school and military service merge. Better to see them on together. An open invitation is extended to join us on our Academic Patriotism radio program, to be announced.

17. Food And Clothing Drives, Across Town

The vehicle(s) must be large enough to hold many items of clothing. The inside of the vehicle must be stable enough, and cool enough, to carry many food items. The "drive" should take the vehicle(s) across the municipality to shelters and other locations where homeless veterans, and others, abide. Ideally, the vehicles will be provided by the military component of the partnership between students and troops.

The determination, as to when food and clothing (and toiletries, and reading material, etc.) drives will take place, should be made by school administrators, in consultation with service cohorts. More, and more, charitable entities are seeking help for those in need during "off" times – when cameras are not rolling, and holiday bells are not ringing. Two elements of the STOOTS for Boots "drives", that make the efforts substantive, are 1.) The fact that the efforts are to occur at "off season" time periods, and, 2) Arrangements are to be made to engage dialogue between students and the veterans who are willing to share their stories.

The cross-town drives afford opportunities for service members (Boots) to mentor students, and for students (STOOTS) to help personnel understand "the world of young people, today." Let us remember, too, that many service members are young, and their exchanges with students may be contemporary. Because of regulations, laws and wisdom regarding health and appropriate interaction, the "drives" must be carefully planned, legally permissible and tightly supervised. Oftentimes, the cameras used to document, and display the activity for positive publicity can be the cameras that monitor, and prevent, unhealthy and/or inappropriate interaction.

STOOTS and Boots do not have to be the planners/leaders of the activity; nor do the participants need to act under the banner of the "STOOTS for Boots" Campaign. The fact that students, and those who teach them, are projecting the association of school leadership with military leadership is enough to help the whole of our society to desire a part in perpetuating this partnership. As food is shared – as the donors and recipients "break bread together" with students learning from veterans – the food will taste that much heartier, and the assist will feel that much more satisfying.

18. Joint Color Guards

JROTC instructors are fantastic role models for their cadets, and for all who observe them in their respective schools. Many students pay little attention to JROTC cadets until they set the stage, and the tone, for school programs by "presenting The Colors." Observers – not just student observers, but many adults and outside guests – take for granted the carrying out of Color Guard duties, as they wait "for the program to begin." Their attitudes are less cynical than apathetic. "This is the way assemblies have begun since I, first, came to school."

Interestingly, even the cynical take little note of the fact that they, themselves, are quiet, respectful and obedient during this traditional ceremony. The reason the young members of the Color Guard are taken for granted is because they do what they do so well. Rare mishaps call attention to their presence. Consistent efficiency causes them to become, almost, anonymous. It is good that we embrace the symbol more profoundly than the symbol bearer. But, we all know how important it is that the symbol be guarded with such care and efficiency that we are not distracted by the surroundings.

JROTC Color Guard cadets must, first, earn the privilege of serving in this capacity. Of those selected, fewer must earn the right to go before their peers – a daunting challenge at any age – and instructors to open a program, or event. Those few cadets must, then, practice over, and over again, to make sure that flags are carried at the proper angles for presentation, weapons are presented appropriately for the commands, until held at "Present Arms!" for the duration of the music, all steps are taken, "in step", every turn is proper, and every placement (the nervous part) of the flags is secure and in sync.

When the audience relaxes, while remaining on our feet as the Color Guard retreats, these wonderful young cadets must maintain decorum until they have reached the rear of the auditorium (or appropriate exit), where they can finally breathe. We never saw them sweat. "No one in the audience" was aware of the fact that someone with a fantastic eye for interior design rearranged the stage after the Color Guard rehearsed, and caused the cadets to have to change their orientation "on the spot." They could not complain, nor could they bow out. The colors must be posted.

Quotation marks enclosing the above phrase, "No one in the audience", suggests, simply, that, yes, someone in the audience did notice; and were impressed. Veterans know when "it's done properly," and they appreciate it. Active duty personnel know when "it's done properly," and they appreciate it. Perhaps joint Color Guard presentations, featuring military personnel presenting with JROTC cadets, can call attention to the great job that is done, consistently, by these students. As is requested, throughout this writing, we seek to have the relationship between study and sacrifice to be conspicuous. Not only will joint presentations of our Colors call attention to the cadets, they will also call attention to our joint military and school leadership missions across the United States of America.

19. Boots and Books Mentoring Programs

Programs. The plural is offered, intentionally. As opposed to requesting that veterans implement, only, the "STOOTS for Boots", Boots and Books Mentoring Program (which we offer to all schools interested), we respect the abilities of districts and schools to fashion your own, such, programs that will be compatible with your landscape. This suggestion speaks, once again, of opportunities to strengthen the relationship between veterans and students; and, to make the relationship visible. The more important consideration is that the program must have substance. The relationship is viable only when students are being helped. In the next chapter, you will read that military members are also helped, as they help, but, here the emphasis is on creating programs that have substantive goals and objectives, a formal relationship between mentors and "partner" schools, a doable plan of action, adequate material and human resources, assessment tools with clearly defined timelines, and openness to parents, guardians and teachers and interested stakeholders. Such programs can be replicated or sustained.

20. Veterans Against Violence

Veterans have seen enough violence. Veterans understand that there are places, and times, where and when violence erupts as a "natural" reaction to wartime circumstances and situations. Even when violent acts are the "expected" behaviors of those engaged for country and/or cause, still, they are unwelcome. The dangers attendant to doing one's duty in battle should never confront service heroes in the neighborhoods where they live, in their own "safe" United States of America. Perhaps hearing from veterans who've "been there, done that", in an authentic theater, for a worthy cause, can help American students think before reacting violently to a minor confrontation.

Forming an organization to address violence – or, joining one – should not set up traumatic scenes for those who have seen enough, already. The idea, here, is to create a non-threatening (either physically or dialogically) forum that will allow students to learn the dangers of putting themselves in self-destructive positions. I coined a term – "huicide" – to suggest that many homicides among young people are very close to suicide, as they knowingly put themselves in life-threatening situations. The bravado they display is difficult for teachers and/or parents to compel young people to abandon. I believe, however, that hearing from those who've had the actual encounter where bravado must yield to one's own, or one's fellow warrior's very survival, might cause local "wannabe's" to consider the larger picture. Fighting for country on the world stage should make "huiciding" for reputation on the streets of small neighborhoods look small, geographically, certainly - but, more so, ideologically (indeed, "ideo-illogically").

Veterans Against Violence may be an organization that invites students to attend monthly forums to discuss how important they – the young people – are (see, "Your country needs you," #12); or, the members of the organization might make themselves available to those (teachers, youth organization leaders, business owners, and others) who need their services. Depending upon the venue, the neighborhood, the partnership with community leaders or the assertiveness of the VAV chapter, confrontations will range from "in your face" to "I'll try putting myself in your place." The image of the group should call attention to how serious things have become. When media promote the presence of veterans in the "war against crime", many people who have paid little attention to the issue, or who thought there was no use in trying to fight it, might very well begin to take notice. Better, still, some new people might get involved in the veterans' efforts with them.

21. "Stars and Skypes" Together

Perhaps a class that is studying current events will incorporate a live report (weekly or monthly) from members of our armed forces ("Stars"). If protocol permits, the reports may come from places where military operations are taking place. Servicemen and women who agree to use Skype technology to interact with students will understand that the primary purpose of the interaction is to motivate students to aim for excellence. The Skype exchanges can come from local VFW posts as well as foreign war zones (when allowed). The likelihood is that students who participate in this activity will approach learning with an attitude of renewed seriousness motivated by their special guests. Of course, the Skype guests may interact with students in various school settings.

22. The Keeping Pace, At Home, Space: TV Challenge.

There are many programs focusing on home makeovers, "flips", rehabs and rebuilds. An addition to this genre of television fare should include a challenging invitation to build a space for students to do homework in the house or apartment where they live. In this particular case, it would likely be in the house or apartment where students, and their siblings, live. Two elements that make this offering unique, and exciting, are: 1.) The construction is to be done by veterans, and 2.) The recipients should be students who live in the most challenging of situations. A selections committee will evaluate requests that are submitted electronically. Selected sites will be shown on the show, which is to air weekly, until it becomes a nightly offering.

23. Academic Patriotism Day

Academic Patriotism Day is a day during which American schools design one activity, or more, to demonstrate their understanding, and acceptance, of the concept. This day should be celebrated at the beginning of the school year. Hopefully, Academic Patriotism Day will become a nationally recognized day celebrated across the country.

24. A's for Wounded Warriors Month

STOOTS for Boots will provide the matrix that records a student's grades and counts the number of A's earned. Using the form, there will be a monetary value attached to each grade of A for every participant who pledges to donate a certain amount per A. If I pledge one dollar for each A earned by a particular student, during the month of October, and the student earns 12 A's, I would pay the Wounded Warriors Project $12.00. While the campaign is run by "STOOTS for Boots," 100% of the donations will go, directly, to Wounded Warriors. The benefit to "STOOTS for Boots" will come in our being able to use another way (added to all the others) to associate respect for American Armed Forces with academics.

25. Student Stars Academic Patriotism Pledge Flag

The STOOTS For Boots website displays our nation's flag. American students are being asked to endorse (meaning, "make') the pledge: **"Because of your sacrifice to defend our nation, I am serious about my education.**

For every endorsement, the student's name will be added to the tally. At the moment a student clicks the "I agree" tab, a star, representing that student's state, will twinkle, and two numbers will be revealed. One number will show the total number of students, up to that point, who have made the pledge. The second number will show the total number of students who have agreed to the commitment from the state of that student's residence. When the flag is fully illuminated, it will indicate that 1,000,000 students have signed on. Another flag will, then, be revealed to begin a new count.

CONCLUSION

Extending the **invitation** to join the academic patriotism campaign expresses the desire to spread the concept of academic patriotism among students and educators throughout the United States. Seeking **engagement** in the campaign takes understanding, and endorsement, of the concept to the level of acting upon that understanding. It is our belief that, once students, educators, service personnel and students' family members become jointly engaged, they will become **excited**, not only about all that the campaign means to our country, but also about the positive relationships that are established while engaged in cultivating a school culture of student excellence backing up military sacrifice. The excitement includes involvement. There are many ways to express excitement beyond those listed, above. Please express your patriotic excitement in your own way.

Epilogue
"Your Boots, Our Books"

American students' parallel patriotism should cause us all to believe, and behave, likewise. When our students shout the slogan, "Your Boots, Our Books – STOOTS For Boots!" as they honor our military at school assemblies, airports, sporting events and other venues, the rest of us should be thinking, "Your Boots, Our 'Business'!" "Your Boots, Our (i.e., Organization's) 'Mission'!" "Your Boots, Our 'Performance'!" "Your Boots, Our Tools!" We should all engage parallel patriotism in honor of our troops.

Do not underestimate the power of American students' serious commitment to excellence. The "Your Boots, Our Books" slogan tells American military heroes that their classroom counterparts in the persons of students and teachers refuse – in a patriotic way – to allow our military to be more dedicated, more focused, more unified, more seriously patriotic on the battlefield than those of us who are in American classrooms. I cannot properly attribute the quote, "There is nothing more powerful than a made up mind", for I do not know its origin. But, as for the sentiment, I can paraphrase with, "We will experience nothing more powerful than the collective patriotic mindset of serious American students." And, their seriousness will compel our entire citizenry to attempt to parallel their dedication.

What does the slogan, "Your Boots, Our Books", suggest? American students realize that service personnel go into every mission with a total understanding of the imperative to succeed.

Failure can mean lost lives, even lost societies. Our young people who shout, "Your Boots, Our Books!" are saying that they go into every class with a full understanding of the imperative for success. Failure can mean lost leadership in innovative productivity leading to lost respect around the world. Students who shout, or utter the phrase, "Your Boots, Our Books!" are students who want our military to know that "they get it." They are saying that there is a parallel between "your fighting and our studying." You do your thing for us on the battlefield knowing that we're doing our thing for you in the classroom. Students greeting heroes who are returning home from distant shores, chanting at airport gates, "Your Boots, Our Books!" are welcoming them with the assurance that "We are not playing in class while you are fighting with class for our benefit."

America should be exposed to such an outpouring of academic patriotism from our young that all of the rest us will feel guilty if we, too, do not exhibit some degree of similar conscientiousness. Ask veteran teachers how long we've looked for a common motivator to excite students across the board to give their best? Many of us have spent careers regretting the fact that so many students, with so much potential, never saw the need to use their gifts to rise to the top and lead others to do the same. Some teachers ask athletic coaches to help them motivate athletes to work as hard in class as they do on the field, the court, the track, the course. Mentors, siblings, celebrities, employers - even gang leaders - have been approached by parents and teachers to motivate, for us, the unmotivated.

The successes we have managed in our efforts to get help are often categorical (e.g., coaches with athletes, employers with student employees, celebrities with aspiring performers, etc.) and

References

[1] *Bible-Based Family Schooling* by Carl R. Boyd Copyright © 2010

[2] The PUSH for Excellence Program of Operation PUSH is now the PUSH/EXCEL Program of the Rainbow PUSH Coalition

[3] US Department Of Education, Institute of Education Sciences, National Center for Education Statistics, 2012 report.

[4] Statistical data from Deseret News National cbaker@deseretnews.com

[5] The Critical Role of Classroom Management by Robert J. Marzano, Jana S. Marzano and Debra J. Pickering, Copyright, 2003, by Association for Supervision and Curriculum Development

[6] New Study Confirms Importance of Teachers by Brian Maienschein, posted December 8, 2010 in the Pomerado News (Poway News Chieftain; Ranch Bernardo News Journal)

[7] Mattie Hopkins at Education Division of Operation PUSH meeting, Chicago, IL, 1973

[8] Web Elements – Home of the periodic table. WebElements: the periodic table on the web, 2014

[9] A Nation At Risk: The Imperative For Educational Reform. The National Commission on Excellence In Education commissioned by Secretary of Education, Terrell Bell, Washington, D.C., 1983

[10] The Holy Bible – 1 Timothy 4:12

[11] Bible-Based Family Schooling, Lesson 47

[12] *Understanding Youth Popular Culture (YPC) and the Hip-Hop Influence* by Patricia Thandi Hicks Harper, Ph.D., President and CEO of the Youth Popular Culture Institute, Inc. Clinton, MD July 2014

[13] ibid.

[14] *Hip-Hop and Youth Culture* by Carl S. Taylor, Ph.D. and Virgil Taylor – Journal of Urban Youth Culture

[15] The Economist, Stars and Swots, "The Learning Curve" (2012), January 19, 2012

[16] Yo Expert Pro Writers Pro Answers – Marian Wilde

[17] Economic Policy Institute, Executive Summary REPORT/ Education *What do international tests really show about U.S. student performance?* By Martin Camoy and Richard Rithstein, January 28, 2013

[18] Education Week (online) July 18, 2014 Quality Counts: *The Global Challenge: Education In A Competitive World* Published In Print January 12, 2012 as Complex Policy Options Abound Amid International Comparisons

[19] The Declaration of Independence, The Congress of The United States of America, July 4, 1776

[20] The Preamble to the Constitution of the United States of America written at the Philadelphia Convention by its delegates, May 25 – September 17, 1787. Information from The National Constitution Center

[21] Guaranteed 4.0 by Donna O. Johnson & Y.C. Chen Copyright 2004 Published by JCYC Studio

[22] Guaranteed A+ Plus by Donna o. Johnson & Y.C. Chen Copyright 2005 Published by JCYC Studio

[23] Outliers The Story Of Success by Malcolm Gladwell Copyright 2008 Little, Brown & Company

[24] ibid. pages 54-57

[25] Challenges and Champions, Urban Education In America – An Educator's Edge Production NSCI 1998

[26] Mountain Gap Middle School Mission Statement Education World www.educationworld.org

[27] Centennial High School www.centennialeagles.org

[28] Avenues – The World School www.avenues.org

[30] The Community Toolbox – The Internet

[31] ibid.

[32] The Holy Bible The Book of James Chapter 2 verse 17 (here, paraphrased)

[33] Plain Teaching 49 Lessons On Becoming A Positive Teacher, Westport Publishers, Carl R. Boyd 1991

[34] ibid.

[35] Edwin Markham, The Creed found in Best Loved Poems of the American People, Doubleday, 1936

[36] The School Liaison Program, Military K-12 Partners, a DoDEA Partnership Program

[37] The Joint Venture Educational Forum Rep K. Mark Takai and Dr. Kathleen Berg, June 21, 2010

[38] Common Ground: Education and the Military – Meeting the Needs Of Students – 2010 Study Group Executive Summary

www.ingramcontent.com/pod-product-compliance
Lightning Source LLC
Chambersburg PA
CBHW071225290326
41931CB00037B/1971